Journey on the Home Front

Books by Arlene Rossen Cardozo

Sequencing (Athaneum/Mac/Millan 1986)

Jewish Family Celebrations (St. Martin's Press 1982)

Woman at Home (Doubleday 1976)

The Liberated Cook (David McKay 1971

Journey on the Home Front

Arlene Ora Rossen Cardozo, PhD

iUniverse, Inc.
Bloomington

JOURNEY ON THE HOME FRONT

iUniverse books may be ordered through booksellers or by contacting:
iUniverse
1663 Liberty Drive
Bloomington, IN 47403
www.iuniverse.com
1-800-Authors (1-800-288-4677)

ISBN: 978-1-4620-0730-1 (pbk)
ISBN: 978-1-4620-0731-8 (ebk)

Printed in the United States of America
iUniverse rev. date: 5/6/11

For Mother and Daddy who made it all possible

For Dick, who makes all that is possible, possible

For Miriam, Rachel and Rebecca, for whom these stories were first written circa 1977

For our future

Joseph

Lerah

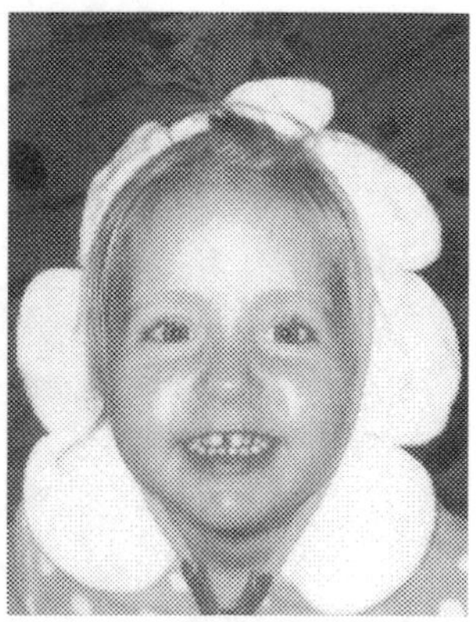

Aurora

"My childhood was as bright and beautiful as the carpet of purple violets on which Mother and I walked on long, lovely summer days…"

Lolly

CONTENTS

PART ONE

A Carpet of Purple Violets

PART TWO

Journey on the Home Front

Acknowledgments

With thanks always to Sally Arteseros, my Doubleday editor for *Woman at Home*, the editor of a lifetime. Sally loved the two examples from my own family included in the book manuscript for *Woman at Home*, and encouraged me to "warm the book up" with some more personal examples, facilitating me while never imposing her own ideas. Following the book's successful media and reader reception, Sally and I talked over lunch several times during the late 1970s and early 1980s about my writing a memoir. She even made comments on an early draft of the first two chapters of what is now this book. But in the 1980s I was raising our growing family, writing other books, making frequent trips to Israel with the family, getting a doctorate, teaching – and somehow the memoir we discussed never happened, at least until now.

I'm also most grateful to my good friend and colleague, talented children's author and educator Bonnie Graves, who read and commented on several drafts, always telling me how much she enjoyed Lolly and wanted me to publish the stories.

My family is the most important part of this book. Most of the stories herein are ones I wrote for our daughters, Miriam, Rachel and Rebecca, over 35 years ago. And the photograph on the cover was taken the summer of 1940 by my mother on her Kodak box camera, as were most of the other photos in the book. Yet who is responsible for these stories now being put into book form? Who else but my wonderful husband Dick, who invested his time and resources throughout; does battle with my computer on my behalf; and laughs on his 100th reading as he did the very first time.

Part One
A Carpet of Purple Violets

My mother Beatrice Ruth Cohen Rossen
and me, Arlene Ora Rossen, a.k.a. Lolly,
Hastings, Minnesota, summer 1940

Chapter One
Hastings – Summer 1940

It was a wringing hot Sunday afternoon. The sun beat down on Mother and me as we walked through a carpet of purple violets, over the hill next to the hospital administration building, and down the circular driveway to our sprawling tudor-style house. The magenta clematis framed the screen porch; the pink petunias which peered out of the second floor window boxes nodded to us as we passed.

"I'll just rest here for a few minutes," Mother said with a sigh as she pulled open the porch door. The heat had turned her brown curls to limp strands; her freshly pressed white smock clung to her body emphasizing the large swelling where her waist had been. I never used to see Mother sit down but now she always seemed to be tired and she napped frequently

"I wonder if Daddy is back yet?" I asked as I ran through the porch and into the living room, looking around for his pipe – always a sure sign that he was home. But I couldn't find it. He had gone up to Cottage Nine hours before, in response to a call from the Supervisor that "Steve is at it again." Steve was a patient who raged in the heat, especially before a bad storm.

Daddy didn't allow patients, no matter how distraught, to be restrained in spite of the employees who complained, "We always tied the patients up until the new Doc came." Although he'd been Superintendent of the Hastings State Mental Hospital for nearly three years – since shortly after I was born – he was still called the "new Doc" by many of the employees, some of whom had worked "out at the State" for nearly fifty years.

When Daddy first took over the hospital he abolished all patient "restraint," a euphemism for beating, then handcuffing, roping or chaining patients, often then throwing them into back wards where they were sometimes left for days at a time. Instead, his mandate was that each patient needed healthy food, daily exercise, and a several-hours-per-week job around the hospital complex so that each felt him or herself a participating member of the community. Some worked on the hospital farm, others in the main kitchen or dining hall, others by keeping up the grounds, or by helping in the offices. Several patients worked in and around our house and were like part of our family.

In fact, Frank and DeWitt had rooms on the lower level of our house, which opened into the huge back yard, gardens and woods. They slept in one of the patient "cottages" and usually came to our house during the day to read, listen to the radio and tend the gardens outside.

Mother lay on the porch glider reading the paper. "Can I go down and play with Frank and DeWitt?" I asked her.

"I know they're here even though it's Sunday because I hear their radio."

"For a little while," she said, "but don't go down until you call them from the top of the stairs and they answer you."

Frank yelled up the stairs as soon as he heard me call his name. "Be right up to get you, Lolly. Stay put until I get there." Lolly was the nickname for Lady La given me by Daddy when I was a few months old and my vocabulary consisted of lalalala sounds.

Frank carried me down on his broad shoulders. He was a serious faced grey-haired grandfather who wore rimless glasses, "For all the reading I do," he told me one day when, as usual, he was engrossed in a thick book. "Want to go out and see if there are any carrots ready to eat?" he asked.

"Sure," I agreed. We walked right out to the yard from the basement and inspected the garden. Frank let me pull up all the carrots I wanted. Then we washed them with the hose, he cut off the tops with his pocket knife and we stood there and ate them.

"Hey, can I join the picnic?" Daddy came up behind us, smiling broadly, and held a hand out to me. But before I could even give him a carrot Frank said, "Doc," and motioned him aside. I heard him say, "DeWitt is having a little problem with the underworld again. We were listening to the baseball game and then he started getting these messages. He's been pretty worried this last hour."

"Hey, DeWitt," Daddy called in the basement door. "What are you staying in there for on such a sunny day? Come on out here for a minute."

DeWitt slowly came into the yard, rubbing his eyes. He was dressed in the white baker's outfit he sometimes borrowed from the main hospital kitchen. He usually looked like a clown in that suit; it set off his reddish face, big round nose and thick-lipped happy smile. But today he looked miserable.

"What's up?" Daddy asked him. "Are you getting those messages again."

"Yes, I am, Doc. Can you call the President? If you'll just call the President and tell him I've had enough; tell him he's got to stop these terrible men or they'll be bothering everybody; they'll take over the whole country soon."

"Yeah, well, it's a concern," Daddy agreed, his blue eyes twinkled but his mouth was set tightly as it always was when he was thinking over a problem. "Now come on up to my den with Lolly and me, DeWitt. We'll call Roosevelt and get it all taken care of."

Daddy's book-lined den with the stone fireplace smelled of his tobacco, and of leather from the black couch. From the window behind his desk I could see the rose and peony gardens down below and the woods and river beyond them. As I watched Frank – who looked like Tom Thumb way down there – picking a bouquet of puffy pink and white peonies, I heard Daddy call the operator of the main hospital switchboard. "Loretta," he said. "DeWitt's having a problem with the underworld again. Will you please get President Roosevelt on the line and tell him to stop those guys. We don't want them pestering DeWitt anymore today. It's hot here and he's got to get some rest."

DeWitt stood by Daddy the whole time, grinning. "Thanks a lot, Doc," he told him. "Last time you called they didn't bother me for over a month. I hope it works again this time."

"It will," Daddy assured him. "Now you better get back and listen to the rest of that game."

"Gosh it's hot," Daddy said to me after DeWitt left. "Let's shut this place up and draw the shades to keep some of that sun out."

"Can we go to every room and count?" I asked.

"Good idea," he replied. "Then we'll be sure we've got all the shades in the house pulled."

Frank had recently taught me to count. I practiced on the rooms of our house. Mother called the house "a monstrosity." Ideally she would have lived in Minneapolis where she grew up, about an hour's drive from the hospital, near her family. Failing that, she would have preferred a small house in Hastings, a mile or two from the hospital, in a neighborhood. But Daddy wouldn't hear of either option. Born and raised in the iron range town of Hibbing, Minnesota, he loved small town life, and believed that there was a "phoniness" to city living perhaps caused, perhaps augmented by the anonymity it afforded people. Besides, in pre-freeway times, the idea of his commuting was not one they ever seriously considered. So Minneapolis was no alternative.

The idea of living in Hastings, off the hospital grounds, was equally repugnant to my father for different reasons. "A doctor belongs with his patients," he said time and again. And he was delighted with the opportunity of living right among his 1,100 patients where "I can keep my finger on things." Thus, the superintendent's residence – located in the heart of the hospital complex and originally built for his predecessor who had nine children – was perfect for him.

Our Hastings house: the Superintendent's residence, Hastings State Hospital

I was glad Daddy felt as he did because I pretended the big house was a castle in which I was a resident princess. Just which princess depended upon what story Mother had most recently read to me. At that moment, although I didn't mention it, I was the Princess Rose Red, as I walked through the house with Daddy, watching him shut windows and draw shades.

Every time I counted rooms of my castle I came out with a different number. That's because I sometimes counted the front hall which was as big as the dining room, and sometimes counted a bathroom or two although Mother said bathrooms didn't count in room counts. When

I counted the front hall and all three bathrooms, and went on all four floors of the house as Daddy and I were doing, I came out with sixteen rooms.

When I added the screen porch off the living room, and the one off Mother and Daddy's bedroom and even the little one off the kitchen, I got nineteen. I never tried to add the attic storage rooms, or mother's big closet with the chair and the window, or the pantry off the dining room because I could only count as far as twenty anyway.

Daddy and I were in one of the second floor guest rooms when the door bell rang. Mother, awakened from her doze on the glider, got to the door before we did. We could hear voices as we started down the steps. Good, it was Uncle John and Auntie Al. They weren't really my aunt and uncle, but they had no children and said I was almost like theirs. And would their own daughter call them Dr. and Mrs. Anderson? I adored Auntie Al who once, even with a broken leg in a full cast, got down on the living room floor and played Tinker Toy with me.

"It was so hot in town," I heard Uncle John telling Mother, "we thought we'd take a ride out and see if it was any cooler here." I had barely run back to my shelf and collected my tinker toy and Judy Puzzles to bring down with me to Auntie Al when the bell rang again. This time it was Daddy's wrestling chum Emerson Hopp, who was so tall he could touch the hall ceiling without even standing on his toes. He drove down from Minneapolis "to get out of that blast furnace."

And so the afternoon went. Everyone, it seemed, who Daddy had ever invited to "drop in and see us when you're out for a ride" – close family friends like Uncle John, Auntie Al and Emerson who frequently did, as well as casual acquaintances whom I'd never seen before – came that afternoon in the hope of finding a breeze.

Daddy had gone to medical school in Minneapolis and did his internship and residency there. A tremendously gregarious person, he had loads of friends in the Twin Cities to whom he was always generously hospitable. People often came and stayed with us, sometimes for days, on little or no notice. And, there was scarcely a meal that we didn't have at least one other person – and generally more – at the table.

So company was nothing new. The only thing that was different was so many people at once, some of whom had never before met each other. And something else was different, too. Usually Daddy invited everybody to stay for dinner. But here it was, getting later, and I counted sixteen people sitting on the porch, on the glider, the swing, the couches and chairs. Nothing had been said about eating. Maybe he didn't want Mother to do all that work; he was always telling her to rest these days.

But she had me to help her. Of course I was pretty busy because everyone was taking a turn playing puzzles with me, or reading me a story. But, in between I helped Mother run back and forth the width of the house to the kitchen to squeeze fresh lemons, take ice from the refrigerator and refill the frosty lemonade pitchers.

All of a sudden, Auntie Al stood up. "Come on, John, it's after 5:30 and we've still got an hour ride back to town." Others began to stir, although some of them looked actually stuck to one another and to the wicker furniture.

How awful if they all left now, just when it was so much fun. Then I'd just have to eat right away and go to bed. "Oh, please don't go. Don't anybody leave." Everyone stopped talking and looked right at me. I stood in the middle of the porch and spoke loudly and clearly. "Won't you all stay for supper?"

I looked at Mother. From the way she squared her shoulders I could tell she wasn't pleased. I don't think anybody else noticed, though, because she smiled at everybody and said, "Oh, yes, please do." And they all did.

Chapter Two
Minneapolis – Late August 1940

The following Sunday Mother wanted to leave for Minneapolis the minute we were awake; then she'd be assured of being a visitor instead of a visitee. But, Daddy had a different agenda. "You just cover your head and get some more shut eye," he told her. "Lady La and I have some important stuff to do."

I followed Daddy to the bathroom where I often sat on the toilet, reciting my newly learned rhymes to him as he shaved. I tried to be quiet so we wouldn't disturb Mother.

"Little Miss Muffet sat on a tuffet, eating her curds and whey…" I recited.

"No, kid, that's not it. Little Miss Muffet sat in a corner eating her cherry pie."

"Wrong, that's Jack Horner," I told him.

"No, it's Miss Muffet…now listen to this. Jack and Jill went down the hill…" he teased in a loud voice.

"They went up the hill, Daddy…"

"How do you know? Now, come on…Jack and Jill sat on a tuffet, then along came little Miss Muffet…" His voice was still louder. Finally he got the reaction he sought.

Mother, who had patiently taught me the rhymes, called from the adjacent bedroom, "Stop it, Ralph. She's proud of knowing them. Why do you have to confuse her?"

"We're just having a little fun in here, now you just leave us alone," he called to her, blue eyes dancing in his white frothy face.

Next, we went out into the upper hall where Daddy did his calisthenics. "How come you do these every day?" I asked as I tried in vain to touch my toes as many times as he did. Although I didn't have nearly as far to go, he was faster.

"I gotta keep in shape," he said. "This is nothing, kid, you should have seen us really work out when I was on the University wrestling team." Daddy had a whole box full of wrestling and football medals that he gave me, not to play with, but to keep and look at. Sometimes, like this morning after exercises, he looked at them with me… "and this is my all University Heavyweight Wrestling Championship Medal for 1930," he said smiling proudly. Then picking up the little good football, his very favorite, he said, "And this is our team football – the Hibbing Junior College State Championship, 1927."

After we put the medals back in their case, we went downstairs, then outside – past the formidable looking orange tiger lilies who seemed to own the hillside and who I often feared would gobble me – down to Daddy's back yard chopping block.

My father Dr. Ralph Rossen, at his chopping block

I never could figure out why, though he chopped at the big block with a heavy sledge hammer every morning, the block never seemed to shrink. When I got bored watching chopping, I swung on my low white chair back swing, pushing myself back and forth with one foot while I counted the oak trees around me.

I could see all the way up the wooded hill from my swing – the administration building where Daddy's office was located right across from our house, the main kitchen and adjacent patient dining hall to its left. I even got a glimpse of Cottage One, the first of the nine red stucco "upper cottages" (patient dormitories) set into the wooded hills.

Finally Daddy finished chopping. "Come on," he said, "You're holding us up. We've got to get the dogs out; you can't just sit there and waste time all day."

Small, wire-haired Timmy bounded out of the basement door and almost knocked me down. Big St. Bernard, Spike, strolled out after we called him twice. Daddy held one leash in each hand; one restrained Timmy and the other tugged at Spike.

Our dogs Spike and Timmy

"Can we go to the farm?" I asked. The farm was up the winding road, past the office buildings and cottages.

I loved watching all the animals – the spotted cows, the dark horses, the chickens in their coop, but most of all I had a favorite pig. I don't know what color he really was because he was always muddy, dusty or both. Since Mother didn't like me to get myself all dirty playing outside, I got pleasure from watching the pig do it.

"We haven't got enough time today," Daddy said, "Let's just walk down to the lower cottages and see what's going on."

We walked a little way before we saw Sparkey coming towards us. One of his eyes looked right at us; the other went sideways.

"Hey, Doc, not so hot out this morning."

"Sparkey," Daddy stopped. "How's that ankle?" It looks like you're walking fine now."

"It's good. I did what you told me. Stopped sitting around and started walking on it every day. You're right, it's stronger."

"He's really a lot better." Daddy said to me after we resumed walking. "When he was admitted six months ago he hardly spoke a word. Now he stopped us first. We'll have him home in another few months."

"Look, Daddy," I interrupted and pointed ahead. "They're not playing baseball yet." The ball park, encircled by the nine orange brick "lower cottages," was empty. Usually, the park was full on the weekends. A team from one cottage would play a team from another while most of the other patients and staff cheered. Each team would argue to have Daddy on its side. Usually, he batted for both.

"Well, it's too early," he replied looking at his watch which he always kept set fifteen minutes fast in the hope of arriving wherever he was supposed to be on time. "Most everybody is still in church."

But somebody was not. "Say, if it isn't Doctor Rossen and Lolly," a heavy jowled lady lumbered up to us. Oh dear, it was Mrs. McGinnis, all dressed up in a pink and white polka dotted suit and wearing a huge red hat with orange poppies on it. She would never stop talking and we would never get to Minneapolis. And Uncle Manuel promised me that if I kept it a secret, he'd have a surprise for me when I came today.

"Maggie," Daddy asked her, "How come you're not in church services?"

"Well, Doctor, God hasn't done anything for me lately. Why should I sit in there on a beautiful morning for Him?"

"Now, Maggie, you know if you don't get in there you'll be sorry all week." Daddy told her. "Come on, Lolly and I will walk you over. Catholic services are in Cottage Eight this morning aren't they?"

"Well, I don't think I'll go, I think I'll just walk along with you." Now for sure we'd never see Uncle Manuel today.

"Maggie, you didn't put that pretty hat on to go walking along the road with us this morning," Daddy told her. By then we were at the entrance of the cottages and could hear the singing through the open doors and windows of Cottage Eight. Maggie cocked her head, looked at us once more, said, "I guess you're right, Doc," and walked right in.

We hurried home. Daddy put Spike and Timmy back in the basement and then took me upstairs to Mother. Her hair was braided across the top of her head. Her pale blue smock matched the blue stitching on her white skirt. "Perfect timing," she smiled at us. "I'm all ready to go."

"I'll just make rounds now, and then we'll be all set," Daddy told her.

Mother groaned. It was 10:30. "Ralph, you know you won't be back until this afternoon."

"It won't take very long," he assured her.

About 1:00 we heard Daddy's booming voice. "Well," Mother said, "it sounds as if he's in Cottage One. If he started at Cottage 18 and worked backward then he'll be here soon."

We often could hear Daddy from the dining room window. While to me it always sounded as if he was in his office in the building directly across the street and up the hill from our house, Mother could differentiate which of the patient cottages he actually was in.

In a few minutes he was at the door. "Come on, why are you two so slow? I wish you wouldn't always keep me waiting half the day," he teased. "Get your sweaters and let's get going."

"Sweaters?" Mother asked him. "It's nearly ninety."

"Yeah, well it might cool down when we're riding home tonight. It never hurts to have a sweater."

I climbed into the back seat of our beige Chevy sedan; it was boiling hot. I rolled my navy blue sweater into a ball, covered it with my scarf and lay down. Daddy opened the windows, and turned on the radio. I looked forward to the cowboy music he always listened to but all I heard as we drove across the old rickety bridge next to our house, was its clatter and creaking, banging and groaning.

**

The next thing I knew we were in front of Grandma Libby's duplex.

Uncle Manuel pulled me out of the car and threw me into the air. "There's a moose in the hoose, get it oot!" he sang. Then he started singing "I love to go swimmin' with bow-legged women and dive between their knees – now don't you go sing *that* song or your mama will give me holy H," he stage whispered, trying to get Mother's attention. But she didn't bite.

"Hey, Bea, feel these muscles, just feel," he stuck out his hairy arm for Mother and me to touch. "Feel this, Lolly, it's like steel," he told me. His flexed arm was hard like Daddy's. "Feel this, Ralph, not a bit of flab, nothing but sheer muscle."

"Settle down, now, Manuel," Daddy told his younger brother. He threw an arm around Uncle Manuel's shoulder. They grinned at each other affectionately. Their father, my Grandpa Abraham, had died when Daddy was a sophomore in medical school and Uncle Manuel was just fourteen. Uncle Manuel always said Daddy had been like a father to him since. The brothers looked amazingly alike and when they were apart were often mistaken one for the other. But standing together, the differences were sharp. Daddy was taller, nearly six feet; Uncle Manuel was slightly shorter and though Daddy's shoulders were broad, Uncle Manuel's were broader. Daddy's hair looked coal black even in the mid-afternoon sunlight and his eyes were bright blue; Uncle Manuel's brown hair had reddish glints, and his eyes, like his hair, were amber. Uncle Manuel's high cheekbones, were like Grandma Libby's – from the Litman side of the family, while Daddy's features as well as his coloring were more like the Romanian Rossens.

"Did you start training yet, Manuel?" Daddy asked him.

"We start tomorrow, but I'm in terrific shape already. I'll be leading the U this season running all the way for a touchdown." Uncle Manuel had me under his arm like a football as he ran all over the yard demonstrating.

"Manuel, you bring Arlene in here, right now," a small voice said from the doorway. He stopped instantly and looked at his white-haired Mother. "We're just having a ball, Mama," he said not even out of breath while I panted. But he brought me right in as she told him to.

Grandma Libby was short and slight, bent over from a back problem and her asthma. She moved slowly and she didn't smile much. Daddy said that before Grandpa Abraham died, she was upright and sprightly, with a sparkle in her eye. But I saw only the serious old woman, who eight years ago moved from their home town of Hibbing to Minneapolis where she was a stranger living near the campus so her children could go to the University. Daddy was in Medical School then, carrying mail during vacations and weekends to pay tuition and help at home. Auntie Ro had just begun college; Uncle Manuel was still in high school. Aunt Minnie was already teaching country school in northern Minnesota, sending home what money she could.

Now, things were easier. Aunt Minnie, Auntie Ro and Daddy were all through school and working; only Uncle Manuel was still at the University, studying business when he wasn't playing football. He and Auntie Ro lived at home with Grandma, in the duplex which they rented in south Minneapolis. Aunt Minnie lived with them during summer vacations when she wasn't teaching.

It was cool and dark inside Grandma Libby's apartment. The mahogany woodwork stood out against the blue patterned walls; the heavy deep print living room sofa and chairs rested on dark carved feet. The large built-in dining room buffet, big oval table and several chairs were all of dark wood. The rugs in both rooms were deep maroon prints.

Grandma Libby's shriveled hands shook as she poured me a cup of cold orange juice. I sat down next to her on the couch to drink it, but just as I began I heard a door slam and Aunt Minnie's voice out in the kitchen. I handed Grandma Libby my cup and ran through the dining room towards Aunt Minnie. "Do you have any paper and crayons today?" I called to her.

"Well, well, well, what kind of greeting is that?" My tall, dark-haired aunt met me in the hall with a very stern expression on her face. I wasn't sure if she was really mad or just pretending but I didn't want to find out. I usually told my other aunts and uncles what *I* wanted to do; but Aunt Minnie told *me* what to do. She taught six grades in one classroom and I heard her say many times that she preferred children who were "mannerly, orderly and well behaved." Whenever she said it, Mother would raise one eyebrow and look me right in the eye as if to say – mannerly, orderly and well behaved – she does not mean you.

"Now, would you like to say hello to me again?" Aunt Minnie asked.

"Hi, Aunt Minnie," I said. "Have you got any paper and crayons for me?"

"Well, that's a little better," she smiled, so she couldn't really be mad. "Yes, of course I've got some things for you." Then she went to her closet where she stored all colors of construction paper, new boxes of crayons, paste, and even scissors and chalk. A minute later she brought me a whole stack of yellow and orange paper. I was hoping for red but I didn't say. And she brought me a whole new box of Crayolas. I went into Auntie Ro's room and lay on her nubby pink bedspread and colored. I hoped she would come home soon and read to me like she usually did. I was so busy that I almost forgot all about the surprise that Uncle Manuel promised me and jumped when he raced into the room

"Hey, sweetheart, let me just tuck you right under my arm. Now shhh…" he whispered in my ear, "don't you tell your Mama or your Papa. You just come on with me and we're going on out with the boys to have some real fun."

"Manuel, you can't take her," Auntie Ro was behind him. "She'll get hurt."

"You just don't worry," he told his sister. "Now we'll only be gone a little while. I want to show the guys my niece. They don't believe me that she's the best looking thing that's ever hit town…I'm just going to take her on over to scrimmage with some of the guys."

I wasn't sure if I'd like that surprise. Scrimmage sounded kind of funny, in fact it sounded like garbage. I had thought a surprise might mean an ice cream cone or a giant almond-studded Hershey bar like he sometimes gave me. But, before I got a chance to wonder much, Mother came into the bedroom, "Come on, Arlene," she told me. "We have to leave now."

"Geeze, Bea, you sure know how to ruin a little fun," Uncle Manuel complained.

He picked me off the bed with one hand, tossed me in the air and caught me with the other. "I'll tell you what I'll do instead. I'm going to get you a seat at the fifty yard line. You're going to be right out there with your Mama and Papa cheering like mad for your Uncle Manuel next month when we open the season. Boy, oh, boy, we'll beat Michigan, we'll beat Wisconsin, we'll win every game and you'll be out there hollering for us…" And he was out the door.

We soon followed. "Ralph, it's after 4 and Mama and Papa have been waiting for hours," Mother told him.

**

Grandma and Grandpa always dressed as if they were going someplace even when they weren't. Though they were just at home, Grandma wore a lavender print dress and shoes with little heels. Grandpa looked like he always did in matching pants and vest, white shirt and a maroon necktie.

They hurried out of the house as they saw our car pull up and were at the curb in time for Grandma to help me out of the back seat. "Dolly, Dolly" she smiled as she scooped me up into her arms. "Come in, come in."

The whole house smelled like cinnamon and apples. "Mama you've been cooking in this heat. You shouldn't have," Mother said. "I told you salad would be plenty."

"Well, I'm not having you drive all this way for some cold potatoes," Grandma told her. "Come, come now Dolly, let's give you some tastes now."

Tastes of the meal to come were synonymous in my mind with Grandma herself. She sat me in my chair at the dining room table, tucked a napkin under my chin, said "we don't want to mess up your pretty dress," and proceeded to feed me like when I was a baby; first one wonderful mouthful and then another. A taste of the chicken soup – there always seemed to be chicken soup at Grandma's whether or not it was a holiday – the finest chicken soup there has ever been; then a bite of juicy brisket, tender carrots, a bit of roast potato.

"You're spoiling her appetite, now she won't eat any supper." Mother lamented but Grandma kept right on feeding me with one hand while waving Mother away with the other. "Lie down, now Ruthie. You look tired. You're going to need a lot more rest now until the baby comes."

My tall, dark haired Uncle Mel strode in just as I was finishing my taste of apple cake, "Hey, kiddo what have you got there?" he asked. Before I could answer he turned to Grandma, "Say, Mama, what was that you told me about not cutting the cake until time for dessert?" Uncle Mel towered over Grandma. She had to look way up to look him in the eye. "That's right," she told him.

"Just a taste," he teased her. "Just a tiny taste?"

"You'll have as much as you want for dessert," she said.

"Uncle Mel, can we play cards now?"

"That depends," he said. "Have you improved any?"

I was hoping he wouldn't remember. He beat me the last time we played. I usually beat everybody else; but

Uncle Mel always beat me. The last time I heard Grandma whisper to him, "Let her win, Melvin," but he shook his head. "She'll never learn then," he replied.

Uncle Mel went to the University Law School and Grandma and Grandpa were very proud of him. "He's at the top of his class," I heard Grandma tell Mother. But Grandpa, who came to this country when he was 15, used to tease Uncle Mel about school. "What do they do, open up your head and put the knowledge in?" he'd ask.

Just then Auntie Ethel hurried in, brown hair pulled back, white skirt swirling. Before she could even blow one smoke ring to me, Uncle Mel asked, "Are you staying for supper or just stopping home between dates?"

"You're one to talk," she answered blowing a smoke ring at me and then one at him too. "Actually I'm just in and out, but I wanted to see Lolly."

"Come on," Auntie Ethel said to me. "I'll race you upstairs." I ran up the stairs ahead of her, got up on her bed and watched while she changed clothes. "What will be it be?" she asked, "this green frock or the yellow one?"

"The yellow, the yellow," I answered as she tossed it over her head and let me try to tie the sash, while she stepped into high-heeled brown sandals.

"Okay honey let's read some stories up here before I go."

"Uncle Wiggily, Uncle Wiggily." I told her. She read lots and lots of Uncle Wiggilys. Then after Auntie Ethel read me *Uncle Wiggily and the Apple Dumpling* twice she gave me a big kiss and said. "Now stay back while I dash down the stairs and out the front door. It's too hot to wear nylons but Mama will have a fit, so I have to get out before she notices."

Chapter Three
Vitamin Poison – December 1940

When Mother went to the hospital to have the baby, Mrs. Mason nearly poisoned me by trying to give me the wrong medicine.

Daddy and Mother left in a hurry. First Daddy woke me and told me that Viola, our housekeeper was sick but, "A nice lady named Mrs. Mason is here with you and I'll be back soon."

I fell asleep again. In the morning Daddy was there with the news that I had a baby sister named Fredrica. She and Mother were fine but they would need to stay in the hospital for a few days. Meanwhile Mother sent love to me and word that I should be good and do what Mrs. Mason told me.

I tried to be nice to Mrs. Mason, but she was not very interesting to talk with and she didn't know where anything was. Also, she was a terrible cook so I ate mostly pancakes; pancakes and syrup…pancakes and jelly…pancakes and butter. On the third morning I heard Daddy tell Mrs. Mason, "Be sure to give Lolly her vitamins." He showed her my vitamin bottle; the only bottle on the second shelf of the kitchen. Then Daddy stood by my small table in the corner of the dining room, pointed at the window through which I could see the big tall building ahead and said "I'll be right across at the office."

Just as I was finishing my pancake breakfast, Mrs. Mason brought me a pill. My vitamins were shaped like little gold footballs; the one she brought in was a round red pill which I refused to take.

"You have to," she said.

"I won't, it's not my vitamin."

"Yes, it is…"

"No, it's not…"

"You take it or I'll hold your mouth open," she threatened as she reached for me.

"Help! Help! Help!," I screamed as loud as I could.

Frank came running from the basement. "What's wrong, Lolly?"

"She's going to poison me with that pill," I screamed.

"Calm down, dear. Mrs. Mason won't hurt you. But I'll go for your father and have him talk to you."

Daddy and Frank arrived a few minutes later. My father's face was white.

"Where did you get that pill?" Daddy asked Mrs. Mason.

"From the bottle you showed me Doctor," she said.

"Please let me see where you got it," he replied.

Mrs. Mason climbed onto the kitchen ledge. Then she reached up to the top shelf where Daddy stored a lot of medicines he didn't want anybody else to use. Mrs. Mason took a bottle from the shelf – four shelves above the one which he had shown her.

My Father's face was red. "Those are not vitamins. They are very dangerous prescription medicines," he told her.

Daddy fired Mrs. Mason. I think he helped her get factory work where, if she sewed the sleeve on where the pants leg should be, it might look funny but nobody would die from it.

Chapter Four
The Movies – Fall 1941

Grandma went to the movies at least once a week. Although she was very busy keeping up the big house on Upton Avenue, cooking delicious meals for Grandpa, Aunt Lucy, Uncle Mel and Auntie Ethel; helping with the Children's Home, the Beth El Women's League, and anyone else who needed her, she always made time to go to the movies. Sometimes she went to a matinee with a lady friend, sometimes she went by herself.

"Grandma, can I go to the movies with you," I asked one day, not at all sure what a movie was.

"I'll take you during the winter," she told me. "Lots of movies I see aren't appropriate for a little girl like you. But a new movie called *Dumbo* is coming in the winter and it will be perfect for you. It's especially for children."

"Oh, good, Grandma," I can hardly wait. "Can we go as soon as it comes?"

"As soon as it comes," she promised.

The next month Grandma called Mother long distance from Minneapolis to Hastings to tell her that DUMBO had arrived in town, and to arrange for me to go with her. They planned that Daddy would drive me to Grandma's house when he went to Minneapolis the following week for a medical meeting. I would stay overnight at Grandma's and the next day we would go out to lunch and the movie.

I was very excited but Mother cautioned me to keep the lunch and movie part of the plan a secret from Daddy, who never wanted me to go to public places. "He won't want you to go because of germs."

I woke up in my bed at Grandma's very early the day of the movie. "We'll lunch at Ivey's a little before noon, and then the matinee is at 1:00," Grandma said. "But what should we do all morning?"

"Can we go downtown early and ride elevators in Dayton's?" I asked hopefully.

"Surely we can," Grandma laughed. "And I think I'll call Dayton's to see if Mr. Weatherwax can give you a haircut while we're there. Your mother will be pleased."

Grandma and I waited for the big yellow streetcar right near her house. She let me put the tokens in the box and take the seat by the window. She even held me up so that I could pull the buzzer-string to let the conductor know it was time for us to get off.

I just loved Dayton's. Grandma told me it was not only Minneapolis' finest department store, but that it was one of the nicest stores in the whole country. I thought it must surely be the very nicest…for could any store be bigger or higher or have more elevators?

"Eighth floor, please," Grandma told the brown-and-white uniformed elevator operator.

"Certainly," the pretty lady replied.

"Oh, Grandma," I said holding my stomach as the elevator went up and up. "Do you think I could possibly become an elevator operator when I grow up? I think it would be more fun than anything in the world."

Grandma squeezed my hand but didn't answer. I sat in the high barber's chair while Mr. Weatherwax cut my curls. Then, we went down the elevator and walked two blocks to Ivey's.

I had heard of Ivey's but never been there. At Grandma's I had eaten Ivey's beautiful white coated candies with the candy flowers decorating the middle and chocolate coated candies with pecans in the center. A dish of Ivey's candies was always in the center of Grandma's high holiday tables. But here in the store were windows and windows of those same candies.

I had heard of heaven. Ivey's must be it. We were shown to a booth. "Grandma, could I just have candy for lunch?" I asked.

"If you want, dear, but I think you should let me read you the menu first. When you hear of all the other things they have, you might not want only candy."

The menu was long and unbelievable. Ivey's had every kind of food I'd ever eaten, and all in sandwiches. There were hamburger sandwiches, roast beef and turkey sandwiches, cheese sandwiches and everything-with-cheese sandwiches. I ordered a club house sandwich. Grandma recommended that we divide one. "They are very big. I'm sure you'll never be able to eat a whole one." But I knew I could and I did.

Ivey's desserts! Never, anywhere else in the world have there been such desserts. Ivey's served sundaes of every variety. I couldn't decide between a hot Uncle Sam and a chocolate flip. “We have to order, dear,” Grandma said, “We don’t want to be late for the movie.”

“I’ll have a chocolate flip this time,” I told her. “Next time a hot Uncle Sam.”

The chocolate flip came in a wide dish. There were scoops of both chocolate and vanilla ice cream with both cherry and hot fudge sauces. It was covered with whipped cream, and marshmallow sauce. And nuts on top and a cherry in the middle.

“Don’t worry,” Grandma said. “You don’t need to finish it all.” But I did, and then asked, “Can I have some candy, Grandma?”

“Let’s buy them to take home and eat later,” she suggested. I ate two of them on the way to the movies. There was a long line in front of the theater. “Oh, dear,” Grandma said. “I hope we can get seats.”

“Will *Dumbo* be elephant color?” I asked Grandma, not at all sure what a movie really was. While we waited Grandma said, “You know, I read that someday there will be machines which we can turn on in our own homes and movies will be shown right there. Also, newscasts and other kinds of programs.”

“You mean like the radio?” I asked.

“Yes, except with pictures,” she told me. “But that won’t be for a long time,” she said. “Right now I’m glad that we have movies downtown. There was no such thing when I was a little girl, or when your mother was little either. I’m so happy that I have the chance to take you to your first movie.”

Inside the theater was dark. Very dark. And it was filled with people. “Grandma, I don’t want to go in,” I told her.

"But darling, the usher said there is still room up near the front," Grandma said. "And the movie is just about to begin."

I held her hand very tightly while we walked down a long dark aisle. She found us two seats in the front row. There were people on either side of us, and also behind us. Some of them were talking; others laughing. It was too dark to see their faces but I was sure I didn't know any of them.

All of a sudden a big lion roared right in front of us. I screamed. Grandma hugged me. "Don't be afraid," she said. "It's just the show beginning." Then a huge elephant's face came at me…and a loud man's voice shouted something about Dumbo, then the big elephant and a little elephant walked towards us…I screamed and screamed and screamed…"Grandma, take me away quick!"

Grandma didn't talk much on the streetcar. I held her hand and ate the rest of the candy. When we got back to Grandma's house Mother was there.

"My goodness," she said. "I just got here and I was going to go down to the store to visit with Papa. I didn't expect to see you back for a couple more hours."

"Oh, Mother," I cried, hugging her. "Movies are just terrible. They are awful. I don't ever want to go to a movie again."

Me, Lolly, atop my pile of leaves, Hastings 1942

Chapter Five
Kathy – Fall 1941

One afternoon as I jumped in the midst of a huge pile of leaves which Big Mike raked for me in back of the Big House, Mother drove up from her every-other-Wednesday bridge club.

"Arlene, come here," she called, "I have something to tell you."

"Just one more jump," I called back, "then I will."

Big Mike laughed as I tried to brush the heavy leaves off my blue windbreaker suit. "Don't you care that I messed them up again?" I asked him.

"I'm glad you did," he told me. "Now I get to rake them all over again. There haven't been many cars here today and I already polished the Chevy twice, so I'm glad to rake."

Big Mike was several inches taller than Daddy, which meant he must have been at least six feet four inches tall. He was very much fatter than Daddy, too. Big Mike loved to wash and polish cars and prided himself on doing a better job than any garage. His secret was "lots of spit." He washed our cars over and over again and also the cars of all of our visitors. Nobody ever asked him, he just did it. Same with raking leaves.

"Arlene, are you coming?" mother called.

"Here I am. What do you have to tell me?" I asked her.

"I met a darling little girl today," she said. "She is my friend Alice Hyland's daughter. Her name is Kathy and she's just one year older than you are."

"How come you never saw her before?" I asked.

"Usually when we have club at Alice's house, the children are at their grandmother's. But both Kathy and her sister Micky were home today because their grandmother had to go to St. Paul."

"Her sister Micky? How funny, my sister is Ricky."

"Kathy is nearly five, a year older than you are. Micky is almost two, so she is a year older than Ricky," Mother said.

"I wish I could play with Kathy," I told her.

"I want you to," Mother replied. "It's not good for you to be with adults so much; you need a child to play with very badly. I'm having club next time and I asked Alice to bring Kathy."

"How tall is she?"

"A little taller than you are."

"What does she look like?"

"She has brown hair and brown eyes like you do, but she wears her hair in long, neat pigtails," Mother said, looking critically at my tangled curls that she liked to keep cut short.

Finally Bridge Club Day came. I spent the morning in a frenzy, taking my toys and games from the shelf in the upstairs hall, to a corner of the dining room, where Mother said we could play.

At last cars began arriving, and the ladies carefully got out, watching not to run nylons or disturb their hats as they left their vehicles. I ran to the door every time the bell rang, even beating DeWitt to it, which was quite a trick. But he was a good sport and waited each time until I'd open the door, to bow and introduce himself, "I'm DeWitt the butler," removing his huge baker's hat (which he borrowed from the cook who ran the main kitchen) each time he did so.

At last, after everyone else was greeted and seated, the Hylands arrived. Alice, tall, erect and beautiful in her navy blue coat and hat, dark hair drawn back in a bun, looked just like a story-book queen come to life. At her side was a little girl. I was so excited that I couldn't contain myself; I burst out of the house and grabbed the little girl's hand.

"Hi, come in and play with me."

Kathy's brown eyes shone, her freckles seemed to spread all over her turned up nose as she smiled and said, "I want to."

"Come and see all my toys," I said as soon as her coat was off. "See, this is my doll Isabelle, and this one is Matilda." I proudly pointed to the dolls with whom I never played. "And this is my new checker game that Daddy got me," I went on.

"Can I play with her?" Kathy asked reaching for Matilda.

"No, no," I shouted, slapping her hand.

"What about her?" she asked shyly.

"No, not Isabelle either…"

"What about the giraffe?"

"No, don't touch it…" I hit her again. Those were all MY toys. Nobody else ever touched them. I didn't want Kathy to touch them – they were mine. Nobody had told me that playing meant somebody else took your things.

The whole afternoon went on in the same way. Each time Kathy tried to play with one thing or another, I slapped her hand or yelled at her. She neither slapped me back nor shouted. She just went into the living room and sat down by her mother at the card table. I followed. "Why aren't you playing with Kathy?" Mother looked up from her cards and asked.

"Because I hate her," I replied much to Mother's embarrassment and the shock of all the other bridge club ladies. "And I want her to go home."

I went into the dining room and sat down on my trike for a very long time. Kathy stayed by her mother in the living room.

At last, the ladies got up from the table, took their hats and coats, thanked Mother and started to leave. Kathy put her coat on, too. Suddenly, I was very, very sorry. I wanted her to stay. "Will you come on my trike with me?" I asked her.

"Yes," she answered. I drove. Kathy stood on the back, arms around me and pushed with one foot. We flew through the big linoleum floored dining room, in and out of the hall where the ladies stood, into the living room and out again.

First I rang the bell. Then Kathy did. Next she drove, and I stood on the back, my arms around her.

The ladies were watching us. They looked surprised. "Kathy, dear, we really have to leave," her mother told her.

"I want her to stay," I said putting my arms around Kathy.

Alice took Kathy by the hand and told us, "You'll see each other again."

We did. But not until ten years later when, on the first day of high school, we happened to sit down next to each other in English class, and as the teacher called out our names we laughed in recognition of each other and in recollection of that afternoon long ago. We have been dear friends ever since.

Chapter Six
The Ring – January 1943

It snowed all night. I know because I got up and looked out the window twice. In the morning, Frank shoveled the snow into huge mounds alongside the driveway. I hurried into my snowsuit and out the front door so quickly that I barely heard Mother call, "Happy Birthday, Lolly."

"Happy Birthday," Frank grinned as I pulled my sled out of the garage and prepared to climb one of the newly formed snow mountains. "How does it feel to be five?" he asked.

"Not too different from four," I told him as I slid down the new mound and on down the hill between our house and the Nurses' Home.

"You wouldn't be expecting any presents today now would you?" Frank teased as I started back up the hill, pulling the rope of my sled behind me.

"Well, maybe one or two," I teased back, knowing I'd get a lot of them. It didn't matter, though, because there was only one thing that I wanted. A ring. I thought about

Arlene Ora Rossen fifth birthday,
Hastings, January 12, 1943

the ring I was going to get from Grandpa all morning as I slid and slid through the bright January cold.

Mother kept calling me, "Come in soon," and then finally, "Lolly, you have to come in right now. It's nearly time for everybody to get here."

At that I rushed into the house and changed into my new red plaid "birthday" dress, white anklets and black patent leather shoes. Oh, why did I slide so long?

I waited by the window until I saw Grandpa's white Buick come slowly down the driveway. "Grandma, Grandpa, Auntie Ethel…" I ran to the door to hug them, "Careful," Grandma laughed as she tried to kiss me while balancing a pile of packages in one hand. "I'll bet you're wondering who these are for?" she teased.

"Hide this, Lolly," Auntie Ethel said handing me a small package wrapped in pretty bright red paper. "Your mother will have a fit. I'll help you with it later." She looked at me in that way she did when we had a special secret from Mother. I knew what was in that package and I could hardly wait. It was nail polish. When Auntie Ethel came she nearly always painted my nails bright red just like hers.

Just then Daddy finally came home from making rounds. "Hey, is it somebody's birthday or something?" he asked, looking around as if he didn't know perfectly well what day it was. We all sat down at the big dining room table. I sat by Daddy.

Grandpa sat at the head of the table. My little sister, Ricky, sat on his lap like she always did and ate peas off his plate.

As soon as lunch was over, Mother brought a huge cake to the table and I blew out all six candles at once while everyone cheered. (One candle was to grow on.)

Then Grandma went into the hall and came back with the stack of packages which she put in front of me. She sat right across from me but I couldn't even see her over all those boxes. It's a good thing, too. Because I was plenty disappointed but I didn't want her to know.

All the boxes were big. None of them was small enough to hold the ring that I'd asked Grandpa for all year. Every time I'd asked, his blue-green eyes twinkled and he said, "Something might be arranged for your birthday."

While he never exactly promised to bring me a ring on my birthday, I was sure from the twinkle in his eyes that he would.

I opened the presents.

Grandma gave me a beautiful new red dress in one box, and in another box a pair of blue corduroy overalls with a white shirt. Great Aunt Lucy sent a pin-the-tail-on-the-donkey game. Mother and Daddy gave me a huge blue book. It was just like the library one Mother always read me. I loved it. It was filled with hundreds and hundreds of stories and rhymes. There were only six pictures, and except for Thumbelina they were all scary. The scariest of all was the one of the two-headed giant. While I was looking to make sure it was just exactly the same as the library book, Mother told everyone, "Now Arlene will have her very own copy and I won't be embarrassed anymore that we're constantly renewing the only library copy."

Such wonderful presents, but what about the ring? That's what I wanted most of all. How could Grandpa have forgotten?

Just as I felt tears start down my cheeks, Grandpa pulled something from his pocket. "Did you think I forgot?" he asked. "I know there's something special that you want." He gave me an envelope. Pretty funny to put a ring in an envelope instead of a box, I thought, as I tore it open. But, there was no ring. Only a piece of yellow paper.

"Do you know what this is?" Grandpa asked me.

"It's a piece of paper," I said, fighting back the tears.

"Do you know what it says?" he asked.

"No…"

"Ralph, will you read it to her?" Grandpa asked Daddy.

"This is a check signed by your grandfather. It says H.B. Cohen right here," Daddy explained. "And look, it says... `pay to the order of' and then your whole name. Then it says, 'In the amount of $5.00.' Holy smokes, Kid, that's a dollar for every year."

Grandpa smiled proudly. "I didn't know what kind of ring you would like best. This way you can go shopping with your grandmother and pick out your favorite ring."

I felt very sad. And, I also felt very mad. What did that piece of paper have to do with a ring? Nothing!

"I don't want any paper," I cried.

"Papa, take the check back," Mother told him. "She doesn't understand at all."

"All right," Grandpa said. He looked unhappy. "I'll take the paper and buy you a ring with it. It might not be the kind of ring you would pick out, but your grandmother will come with me and we'll do the best we can."

The next week when we went to Grandma and Grandpa's house in Minneapolis, Grandpa handed me a small box. I pulled it open. There was the most beautiful ring in the world. It was gold with a red stone in the center. "It's your birthstone," he told me.

"Oh, Grandpa, I just love it. Thank you. Thank you."

He hugged me, then he shrugged his shoulders and looked at Mother. "She could have bought five rings with the check."

"But, Grandpa, I don't want five rings," I told him. "I want only this ring." I put it on my fourth finger but it was too big; then I put it on my middle finger and it was just right. "I'm never, ever taking this off," I told him.

Chapter Seven
Leaving Home – April 1943

Trunks, boxes and suitcases lined the front wall of our long living room. Some were marked "attic," some were marked "Minneapolis" and a few were marked "D.C." Frank and DeWitt helped Daddy carry those marked "attic" to one of the third floor storerooms.

Daddy was leaving for Washington, D.C., early the next morning to join the Navy. Mother, Ricky and I were going to live with Grandma and Grandpa in Minneapolis until Daddy found a place for us to live there.

A steady stream of people came and went all day; the telephone rang constantly. Family, colleagues, employees, patients – everyone wanted to say goodbye to Daddy and to wish him well. Everyone who was not already in the service, that is. Uncle Manuel left months before and was somewhere in the South Pacific. Emerson Hopp hadn't wrestled with Daddy in over a year; he'd enlisted, too. Chuck Frawley, the freckle-faced hospital recreation director, who had gone with the first call-ups, was killed in an early invasion. His wife was left with four small children, among them Billy who was just my age.

Daddy frantically tried to get into the service for nearly a year. The Army stamped him 4-F because of poor eyesight. He agitated to take the eye exam again; and flunked it again. He was furious. "Those no good SOB's, what do they know about it, anyway? My eyes are just fine."

He had proof. On the fourth of July 1942 just before he took the first eye test, the boys from the Red Wing Reformatory joined the patients at our hospital for their annual baseball game. Daddy stood by the bleachers talking with the team captains just before the game began. Two of the Reform School boys sauntered up to him. The tall redheaded one was holding a football. "Say, Doctor," he said. "All we ever hear from these Hastings guys is what a great athlete you are. Would you show us?"

"What did you have in mind?" Daddy asked.

The short pug-nosed boy answered, "We was just wondering if you'd mind kicking this here football down through that basketball hoop?" He pointed to a basketball hoop way across the park.

"That's about fifty yards from here wouldn't you say?" Daddy asked nonchalantly as he caught the football the tall boy tossed him, winked over his shoulder at Mother and me, then kicked the football right through the hoop. A legend was born. No one was more surprised than

Daddy. All assembled that day testified forever after to his phenomenal coordination, aim and eyesight. Unfortunately there was not an Army recruiter among them.

After badgering everyone he knew in the Army to help him get in, he directed his efforts to the Navy. At one point the Governor of Minnesota intervened. Not to help get Daddy in but to keep him out. The Governor declared him "Essential to the state of Minnesota," saying "As a doctor in charge of 1,100 patients Dr. Ralph Rossen's services are necessary at home."

Daddy ignored his exemption. Yes; he hated to leave us and he hated to leave his patients. No, he would not stay back. He continued to pull every string he could until finally his good friend and colleague Dr. Herman Hilleboe, then with the U.S. Public Health Service, convinced an admiral to request Daddy's services for the U.S. Navy.

"I still can't understand your doing this, Ralph," Grandpa told him when he came to say goodbye.

Nobody seemed to understand it but Daddy, and maybe Mother who, while she supported his decision, or at least realized she was powerless to keep him back, didn't like it either.

"Look," he tried once again to explain to Grandpa, "the Nazis are overrunning Europe, and if they win they'll be here next. I've got to help keep our country for our children."

"Fine, Ralph," Grandpa argued, aware that Daddy's orders were in his pocket and that no discussion would help at this point, anyway. Yet he seemed to need to express his dissatisfaction once more. "But, there are other Americans who can go – younger men, you're 32; single men, you're a father; unskilled men, you're a doctor, needed here – even the Governor says so. Why would you risk leaving your children fatherless and Bea a widow when you don't have to?"

"But I do have to HB, you should understand this better than anyone else," Daddy got up from the table where we were all sitting, and paced around the dining room. "You know what's happening to the Jews in Europe; you've still got cousins there, or you did anyway before the Nazis started their massacres. No American Jew should sit and watch from the sidelines."

Grandpa was silent. His heavy dark brow was furrowed above his cloudy looking grey-green eyes. He twisted the chain of his large gold pocket watch as Daddy continued. "And even if I could rationalize staying home as an American – which I can't – I clearly cannot stay home as a Jew."

Daddy had already gone over the same ground with his own mother when we were there the night before. Worry did not help her failing health and he felt guilty knowing that with Uncle Manuel already at war his absence would bring additional strain on her. He had tears in his eyes when he held her fragile body against his and kissed her goodbye. He didn't talk at all in the car on the way home.

Leaving all of us – especially Mother, Ricky and me – was terribly hard for him because he hated ever to leave us.

A few months before, he had driven off early in the morning for a medical meeting in St. Louis – almost 800 miles away – only to return home shortly after lunch. "It's not worth it," he said, kissing us all. "What do I have to run down there for and be away from all of you for a week?" But in this case, commitment to what he thought was right took precedence over his emotions. He tried to explain this to Ricky and me when, at sunset, we went out for our usual before bedtime walk.

"Someday you'll understand," he told us. "You'll never have to be ashamed and make excuses for why your father didn't help fight this war." Ricky yawned. Daddy picked her up and carried her in one arm, while he held my hand with the other. "You'll have to take care of yourself, kid," he told me, "and watch over your sister, too. And help Mother all you can."

He sounded so wistful and he had a faraway look in his deep blue eyes. We were almost back at the house. It was an unusually mild evening. Daddy sat down on the cement ledge overlooking the back garden; Ricky crawled off his lap. I got on his lap and then held her in mine.

Daddy holding me, holding Ricky,
before he left for the Navy

I did not want my father to leave. And, I didn't want to leave Hastings, either. This was my world. The world Daddy ran. Maybe something would happen to keep him here. Then he would not have to leave. Suddenly, I had a wonderful idea. If I lost my ring, Daddy would not be able to leave; he would have to stay and look for it.

I slipped my precious red ring off my finger. It was the first time I'd taken it off since Grandpa and Grandma gave it to me. When I moved my arms from around Ricky she scooted off my lap. Daddy ran after her. I loitered by the little patches of lilies of the valley at the porch side of the house. Then I ran ahead to join Daddy and Ricky, stopping briefly to slip my ring under a small rock.

"Daddy, Daddy, I lost my ring. My beautiful red ring," I cried.

"Come on, Rick, let's help Arlene look for the ring," he said.

We looked in the rose patch, and behind the fir trees, under each violet, in the clover. But we couldn't find my ring anywhere.

I thought that I knew exactly where I'd put it, but there were lots of rocks on the ground and besides it was nearly dark.

I clung to Daddy terrified at what I had done. I might never see the ring again; I might never see Daddy again. I cried hysterically.

"Take it easy, kid," he comforted me. "I'll get you a new ring as soon as I get to Washington." But I could not be quieted. I felt too guilty about hiding the ring and too frightened at the thought of Daddy's leaving us and of us all leaving Hastings.

"He'll get me a new one in Washington," translated to "I'm going anyway."

"He is going anyway," I thought. "So why, oh why did I give up my ring?"

"Come on, let's take one last look," he said. "Now, think real hard about just where you were when you last had the ring," he told me. "Go back to where you were sitting and retrace your steps. I'll take Rick in and get a flashlight."

I went back to the ledge and sat down. Then I got up and walked to about where I thought I was when I removed the ring. I bent down and looked and looked but still no ring. Then Daddy came out. We searched everywhere with the flashlight. I held it and Daddy looked behind every bush and flower, and lifted every leaf and rock until at last something reflected in the light and he cried out, "Hey, kid, what's that?"

"It's my ring, my ring," I rejoiced. "Oh, Daddy, you found my ring, my ring is back." I thought for a minute and then asked, "Will you come back just like my ring did?"

He picked the ring up and put it in my hand. "I promise. Someday this war will end and I'll come back."

Part Two
Journey on the Home Front

Arlene Ora Rossen in our Chevy coupe, April 1943

Chapter One
The Porter – Late April 1943

A couple of weeks after Daddy left, Mother came running into our bedroom at Grandma's house, waking Ricky and me. She was flushed and talking rapidly. "Your father has found us an apartment in Washington. He doesn't know how long he'll be stationed there or where he'll be sent next but he wants us there with him. We're leaving as soon as we can get reservations."

The following week, Grandpa took Mother, Auntie Ro—who agreed to help Mother on the long train trip with us—Ricky, Teddy (her bear who went everywhere with her) and me to board the train. Grandpa's grey-green eyes had tears in them, and Mother's cheeks had tears running down them, as we hugged Grandpa goodbye at the bottom of the steps to the train. All of a sudden, there was a huge rumbling noise, and a loud whistle.

"All aboard that's going aboard," the Conductor called.

Mother picked Ricky up, Auntie Ro grabbed my hand and we hurried onto the train.

Ricky and I had never been on a train. Mother quickly found a row of seats and sat down with Ricky on her lap. Auntie Ro sat next to her. They left the aisle seat for me.

"Sit down," Mother cautioned me, "The train is about to start."

Everybody else in the train was seated. But I was too excited. I hopped up and down in the aisle until the last whistle blew, and I was jolted onto the lap of an unsuspecting young soldier.

"My goodness," he said, "I wasn't expecting company." I started to get up, but the train jerked and I flew back onto him again.

"I'm so sorry," Mother called over to him. Then she put Ricky onto Auntie Ro's lap and came over to retrieve me. She took my hand and lectured me, "You've got to sit right where I tell you and not get up except when you hold my hand or Auntie Ro's hand."

Just then, the porter came to ask if we needed anything. Ricky screamed and screamed. "He's dirty, he's dirty."

"No, he's not," Mother told her. "He's a colored man."

"I'm sorry," Mother told him. "We live in a small town and my little girl has never seen. . . "

"That's all right," he smiled so kindly. "It's natural for her to cry when she sees somebody she hasn't seen before."

"Thank you for being so understanding," Mother told him.

Ricky continued to scream whenever she saw him. Mother explained to me that Ricky was scared because she had never seen a Negro before. I hadn't ever seen one either, but I didn't see anything to scream about. He was just a man.

"Do you happen to play gin rummy?" I called across the aisle to the soldier with the nice lap. All the other soldiers around him started laughing.

"Sure," he said laughing, too. "Come on over, I'll challenge you to a match."

He was pretty good. We played until the porter came through the aisles shouting, "First call to lunch, first call to lunch."

"I have to go to the dining car," the soldier said.

I went back over to Mother, "Can we go to the dining car, too?" I asked.

"Shush, sit down now. No, I made us some peanut butter and jelly sandwiches and a thermos of milk. We don't have to eat in the diner," she said.

Don't *have* to eat in the diner? What could be more glamorous than eating in the dining car? I begged, I nagged and cajoled, but to no avail.

"The dining car is very expensive," Mother said, "It's bad enough that we have to have dinner there." So it was peanut butter and jelly, the very same as if we'd have stayed at home.

We changed trains in Chicago. Somehow, though the train was packed with soldiers with very few civilians on it, Daddy had arranged a compartment. I was delighted with the tiny room.

"Mother, can you and Ricky please sleep on the bottom and let Auntie Ro and me get the pull out top?" I asked.

"That's just what I planned," Mother assured me, as Auntie Ro groaned.

Just then the conductor came in to check tickets. "Stay here now," he said, "we pull out in about 15 minutes."

All of a sudden Ricky started to wail. "Where's Teddy? Where's Teddy?"

"You were carrying him off the other train," Mother told her, "Don't you have him now?"

"Teddy gone, Teddy all gone," she cried. "I go get Teddy."

"You wait here," Mother told the three of us, "I'll run back to the other train and try to find Teddy."

"You'll never get back here, Bea," Ro warned, "And I don't relish going all the way to Washington alone with these two."

"We'll all go to the other train," I suggested, "So if we don't get back here in time, we can be together."

"That's impossible," Mother told me. "It could take weeks to get new reservations, and we have nowhere to stay in Chicago. We'll simply have to get another Teddy when we get to Washington."

"No other Teddy," Ricky cried, "No other Teddy."

Just then there was a knock at our compartment door. I opened it. Ricky screamed. It was the porter from our other train.

"Miss," he said, "Don't be scared. Look, don't this bear belong to you?"

Ricky grabbed Teddy. Then she grabbed the porter's leg and smiled and reached for him to lift her up. He did. She hugged him. "I just love this man," she said. Just then the whistle blew and the train jolted.

"Whoops, miss," the porter said, giving Ricky back to Mother. "I got to get off of here and back to my other train. You all have a safe trip."

I stood in the doorway of our compartment watching him hurry away. Just as he was nearly out of sight, he called back to me, "Now, you make sure to help your sister take care of that bear."

Chapter Two
On the Train to Washington

"First call to dinner; first call to dinner..." The conductor's voice was loud and clear.

"Do we get to go right now?" I asked Mother.

"Ricky fell asleep," Mother said. "I'm going to stay here and order from room service. I'll order food for her, too, in case she wakes up. Ro, what do you want to do?"

"I'm happy to stay in here and eat..."

"Oh, no, oh, please Auntie Ro, let's go to the diner, the diner will be much better, please..."

Auntie Ro looked from Mother to me. "I'll go to the diner with you if it's okay with your Mother."

"Fine," Mother said, "you can go to the diner with Auntie Ro. But be quiet and mannerly."

I was out the door of the compartment and halfway down our car before Auntie Ro caught up with me. "Please stay right with me," she said, "I don't want you to get lost."

"I couldn't possibly get lost," I told her confidently. "I know that we're in Room B."

"That's right," she told me, "but the diner is many cars away and there might be lots of Room B's."

"I doubt it," I said airily.

We went through one car and then another. The cars nearest to us were also bedroom cars. And every one of them had a Room B. Then we walked through the coaches. Finally, we came to a long line of soldiers. The tall frecklefaced soldier at the back of the line said, "Chow's ahead."

"That means we've finally gotten to the right place," Auntie Ro told me. We waited and waited. At last, the dining steward said "Come right this way," and he showed us to a table.

It was hard to decide what to order. Everything on the menu looked wonderful. "Chicken? Hamburger pattie? What will you have?" Auntie Ro asked me.

"Where do you see those?" I asked her. She pointed to one side of the menu. I couldn't read the words but I saw that there was a drawing of children by the hamburger pattie. "Is that the kids' side?" I asked her cautiously.

"It says: 'Children's portions,'" she told me.

"I don't want children's portions," I said. "I want just what everybody else on this train gets. Not what they have for children."

The waiter heard us. "Children's portions is just the same as everybody on this train gets," he told me, "but less of it."

"I want the same amount as everybody else," I told Auntie Ro. "What are you having?"

"I'm having chicken," she said. "Now you had better decide and not keep the waiter standing here. There are many soldiers waiting for their dinner."

"I'm having two lamb chops," I said importantly, "with mashed potatoes and carrots."

"Your Mother won't be pleased when she finds that you ordered the most expensive thing on the menu," Auntie Ro told me. "At least you'd better eat every bit of it."

The train rocked back and forth, stopped, then moments later jolted ahead. I ducked down because I thought for sure the waiter was going to drop the whole tray he carried high above his head, balanced on one hand, on me. He just laughed. "We get used to those quick stops," he said. "I've never dropped a tray yet and I've been doing this job for 22 years."

"The train will be bouncing around for a little while," he added. "They're just changing some cars." I wasn't sure what that meant, but I didn't ask because I didn't feel much like talking.

Eating in the diner wasn't so nice as I had expected. It was crowded and noisy. The train stopped and started, rocked and jolted. Everything smelled funny. My lamb chops weren't tender like the lamb chops in Hastings. They were tough and hard to eat with a fork. Auntie Ro wouldn't let me pick them up. "They're way too big to pick up," she said. "You're in public and you must cut them into little bites. Here, let me do it for you."

Even after she cut them they were still tough. And, the mashed potatoes had some horrid stuff on them the waiter called gravy. They gave me only two little pieces of carrot.

I ate them. But not the potatoes with the terrible brown stuff on them; and not those hard-to-chew chops.

I could hardly wait to get back to our room to see my Mother and tell her how bad it all tasted. "Come on, Auntie Ro, let's hurry," I said as she drank her coffee. And when she didn't get up I added, "there are lots of hungry soldiers waiting for our table."

I ran out of the dining car, past the line of waiting soldiers. "How was dinner?" a short red-headed one asked me.

"Just awful," I replied.

"You should taste Army chow," he told me. "Then I bet you'd like your dinner here."

I ran through car after car. Auntie Ro huffed and puffed, as she hurried after me. Every time she caught up with me she said, "Slow down."

I started crying. I was never going to get back to Mother. I could tell I wasn't because there were only coaches and more coaches filled with talking, smoking, laughing soldiers. There weren't any sleeping cars. That must be what the waiter meant when he said, "They're changing some cars." They must have taken the sleeping cars away and changed them to another train.

"Mother, Mother," I called, "Mother, Mother...dinner was terrible, and I only ate three bites of lamb chops... Mother, Mother, I ate only two little carrots."

At last, after another coach and another coach I got to a bedroom car. I pounded on the door to Room B, but the man who answered was not my Mother. "Excuse us, Sir," Auntie Ro said as she caught up with me. She pushed me ahead of her with one hand, held onto the back of my collar with the other. "We're three more cars down. Now don't you dare knock on any more doors, and for heaven sakes stop crying before we get to your Mother."

But I didn't stop crying. And, when I got to Mother I cried all the harder, because she and Ricky were sitting in the compartment happily eating ice cream.

Chapter Three
The Apartment – Late April 1943

"Boy, oh boy, is it good to see you again," Daddy hugged me and kissed me. I kissed him on both cheeks. The shaving cream smelled like Daddy, and the bright blue eyes smiled like Daddy, even though he sure didn't look like Daddy in that uniform.

Lieutenant Ralph Rossen MD
in his Naval uniform

"Come on, let's get you out of here," he said to us. "Did you get any sleep at all?" he asked Mother, as we walked out of the station.

"It was really very comfortable," Mother said. "Ricky slept most of the night curled into a little ball."

Auntie Ro lit a cigarette. "You didn't ask me."

"Well?" Daddy looked at her.

"Well?" Auntie Ro looked at me.

"Well," I said as we got into the car, "Auntie Ro says the bruise on her leg is from my kicking..." They all laughed.

So this was Washington. It didn't look very different from Minneapolis to me. But Mother thought it looked much different. "Look at the magnificent trees," Mother exclaimed. "They're flowering already and it's barely the end of April."

"Here's our apartment complex," Daddy said after a lot of driving. "You can't believe how hard it is to find any kind of housing here. There are waiting lists many months long. We're really lucky."

Ahead of us were lots of reddish-brown buildings. Mother had said that our apartment would be very small. But none of those buildings looked small. Each of them looked much bigger than our big house in Hastings.

"Here we are," Daddy said, stopping the car. "This is where we'll park. And that's our new apartment building. Let me get you in first, then I'll come out and take the bags in."

There were many mailboxes inside the apartment building. "We're on the second floor," Daddy said. "I tried to get first floor because of Ricky — I don't want her on steps, but there just wasn't anything available. So we can never leave our door open. Don't take any chances, not even when she's in her crib."

We walked up a flight of stairs. How funny, I thought. I never heard of going into the house on the second floor. Daddy opened a door. "This is it," he told us.

There was a living room with a dining room table in one corner, a kitchen, a bathroom and two bedrooms. "Ro, this couch opens into a bed," Daddy told her, "You can either sleep out here, or we can get an extra cot and put it in with the kids."

"But what about all the other rooms in the house?" I asked. "Why can't Auntie Ro have one of them?"

"What other rooms? This is it," Mother said. "And it's much larger than I expected. It will do very nicely."

"But this whole apartment building...it's a big building... what about all the other rooms? Why can't we go in them?"

Mother and Daddy and Auntie Ro looked at one another. They smiled, "Kid, lots and lots of other people live in this building, too," Daddy said. "We have this part of the building, and other families have other parts of the building."

Oh, so it wasn't just our house. Lots of other people were going to live there with us.

"Come on down with me," Daddy told me. "You can help me bring the suitcases in." When we got outside he said, "There's something I want to show you," and he pointed ahead of us. "Look, kid," he said.

Right out in the middle of all the buildings was a big playground. Children were swinging, some were teeter-tottering, and others were on the merry-go-round. Some big kids were playing ball off to one side, and some little ones, about Ricky's age, were in a sandbox.

"Doesn't that look like fun?" Daddy asked. "And right in your own backyard."

The swings did look like lots of fun except for all the kids who were on them. I thought longingly of the swing in our backyard at Hastings. It was all mine. So was the teeter-totter. Only Ricky went on it with me when Mother held her. We had our own sandbox at home, too.

"Should we go over and I'll push you?" Daddy asked.

"I think I'll wait until tomorrow," I told him. "I don't feel much like swinging now."

I got up when Daddy left early the next morning. I could see the playground from my bedroom window. Hardly anybody was out there. Two swings were empty. I hurried into my clothes and put on my yellow jacket. "I'm going out to swing," I told Mother.

"I don't think you'd better go alone," Mother said. "Wait just a little while and I'll take you. I'm not sure you'll find the way back."

How silly of her! Of course I'd find the way back. How could I not? The playground was right behind the building. "Of course, I'll find the way back. I know what our building looks like," I told her.

It's a good thing I got out when I did because I got the last swing. I swung and swung. It felt good. It was warm in Washington. At home I might still be building snowmen.

When I got tired of swinging, I went over to the merry-go-round, but kids were pushing it too fast and I couldn't get on. Some kids were playing a game right near me. It was called "Duck, duck, grey duck."

"Do you want to play?" a blond-haired girl asked me.

"Sure," I said. But nobody picked me for grey duck. Nobody picked her either.

"I have to go," she said. "Bye." And she ran off.

I felt hungry so I left, too. I hurried toward our building. Or was it our building? The apartments formed a circle with the playground in the middle. I could see the swings from my bedroom window. So then, I told myself, all I had to do was look up and find my bedroom window. But, all the windows looked alike, and they all faced the playground.

I knew our apartment number was 201, so I figured I'd just go into 201. I ran into the building closest to me and up the stairs to 201. A nice dark-haired lady answered but she wasn't my mother. "I'm sorry," she said. I said I was, too, and left in a hurry.

I tried the next building. The man in 201 wasn't very nice. He said I woke him. Then I got scared. Suppose I couldn't ever find our building? I ran from building to building, knocking on 201's. Most of the people were very nice, some weren't home, and one man was mad. "I've got the flu," he said, and slammed the door.

I went back out by the merry-go-round and stood there. The sun was shining but I felt cold. Then I started to shiver. Suppose I could never find our apartment again? Suppose I had to stay outside alone all night? Suppose.... Just then I saw Mother and Ricky walking towards me. I pretended not to notice them. When they got closer, I waved. "Hi," I said. "Should we teeter, Ricky?"

Chapter Four
A Very Temporary Dwelling – Early June 1943

By the time I found my way from our apartment to the playground and back again it was time to move. "Daddy got orders this morning," Mother told Ricky and me at lunch. "We are moving to Richmond, Virginia, in ten days."

"But we've only been here for a month," I said.

"This is the Navy," Mother replied. "We're lucky that Daddy didn't get shipped out. He will be stationed at Camp Peary, not too far from Richmond. We can follow him to Richmond. If we can find a place to live there, that is...."

Daddy went to Richmond on his day off for the whole day. When he got home he told us he found us a place to live. "Temporarily, for a couple weeks, until we can find something."

"What's it like? Tell me."

"It's a surprise," he said. "But you'll like it."

Our temporary place was called a plantation. The house was even bigger than our house at Hastings. And, the grounds were huge, too. There were magnificent gardens, beautiful bright flowers, blazing vines and flowering trees bloomed everywhere.

"It's nothing like it used to be," Hezekiah told us. Hezekiah was very, very old. He had dark skin and white hair. "This used to be a cotton plantation. Before the War cotton was growing everywhere."

It was hard for me to imagine it all covered with cotton just the year before. But World War II wasn't the war Hezekiah meant. "Back when I was your age," he told me, "my family was slaves. We used to live way down behind this house, and my father worked in the cotton fields all day."

"Then came the War and the cotton fields was all burned down. After the war we slaves was free. All the other darkies left, but my father and mother stayed right here and I stayed, too. They died a long time ago but I stayed on here with the Robbs. The Robbs are all dead now, too, except for one. And I take care of him just like my family always done."

The surviving Robb was at least as old as Hezekiah. Mother said that they both must be nearly ninety years old. She also said Mr. Robb used up most of his money and that's why he took in boarders. But he hadn't ever had any boarders like us.

"You're Yankees and besides that you're Jews. I just don't know...," he had told my father, when Daddy first came in search of a place.

Daddy, desperate to find somewhere to house us until he could find something else, persuaded him.

We had our own living quarters. Mother wasn't allowed in the kitchen. "None of our boarders is," Hezekiah told her. “The cook has done things her own way for fifty years now, and it’s just the way her Mama done them before her. “So you just come to the table when I ring the dinner bell and that’s all you has to do.”

Mr. Robb didn’t come to the table very often. Hezekiah brought him meals on a silver tray. Often I saw Hezekiah bringing the tray back to the kitchen again with everything still on it, saying, “He is ailing today.”

Sometimes we got to go into the main parlour. It was tremendous. “Don’t sit on anything,” Mother said, “You can look but don’t touch and don’t sit. These things are antiques. They’ve been here since before the Civil War.”

One afternoon when Mother was talking to Hezekiah outside the front door Ricky and I went into the house without her. Nobody was around. The cook was in the kitchen. Mr. Robb must be upstairs ailing, I thought.

“Let’s go into the parlour,” I said to Ricky.

“Just look,” Ricky said.

“We’ll just look,” I agreed.

There was a certain couch in the parlour that intrigued me. In fact, it wasn’t really a couch, but it wasn’t a chair either. It was a triangular shaped piece of furniture the likes of which I had never seen. The frame was made of dark, carved wood; the upholstery was bright green. There were places for three people to sit. Each place looked like a chair, but because they were all attached, it also seemed like a couch. How on earth could people seated there talk with one another? Wouldn’t they see only the backs of each others heads?

I had to find out. “Ricky, come here,” I told her, “over here by this.”

“Only look,” she said.

"Only to look," I agreed.

But even when we got very close I couldn't figure out how the seating would work. And I had to know.

"Ricky, sit here for a minute," I pointed to one of the three seats. "Come on, it will be okay. Only for a minute."

"Not touch," she said.

"Not touch, just sit," I told her.

"Not sit, not touch, only look."

"Yes, sit, sit now. It's okay because I said so."

My authoritative manner calmed her concerns. She sat. So did I. We couldn't possibly talk to each other because we couldn't even see each other over the high backs of each section of the furniture—couch or chair, whatever it was. So I had to stand up on it. But even then I couldn't see Ricky.

The only way to tell about how this piece of furniture worked as to get on to the third part. So I had to half walk, half crawl around on it. But even on the third section, I still couldn't see Ricky.

"You better stand up on the seat so I can see you," I called to her.

She did. "Now, be careful," I commanded, "and come over next to me."

She held onto the back and walked all around to me. She didn't even fall once.

This must be a kind of merry-go-round couch, I thought. Maybe other people did just what we did, tried all the different sections and didn't really sit and talk at all.

What a wonderful piece of furniture. Maybe we could find out the name and get one for our house in Hastings.

"What is going on in here?" boomed an angry voice. It wasn't Hezekiah—it was Mr. Robb.

"Nothing," I quivered.

"Just look," Ricky said.

Mother and Hezekiah ran into the room. "I'm terribly sorry," Mother told Mr. Robb. "They have never been on the furniture before, and I assure you it won't happen again."

It didn't either. Two days later, Daddy found us our very own house which we rented for the remaining six months we lived in Richmond. It was tiny. But we got to sit on the furniture.

Chapter Five
Richmond – Late June-December 1943

The best thing about our tiny new white house was the guest room. That meant Auntie Ethel would come and visit us, as soon as she finished teaching her kindergarten classes and school was out for summer vacation.

I impatiently counted the days until my high spirited, brown-haired, brown-eyed Auntie would arrive. I had such wonderful memories of Auntie Ethel's visits to Hastings, when she would tell me stories while painting my nails bright red like hers. But my very best memories were of staying overnight at Grandma's house, and sitting right in the middle of Auntie Ethel's bed watching her get ready to go to parties with her beaus. I'd get to hear all about where she was going, and the next day I'd hear about the beautiful dresses everyone wore. Now that she was coming to Richmond I'd get to do that every day. I could hardly wait!

At last she came, followed by the U.S. Army. "Ethel, we planned to meet your train in another hour," Mother said when she answered the doorbell and saw her sister. "How did...?"

"This is Paul," Auntie Ethel said, "and this is Sam... we met on the train from Minneapolis to Washington. Paul had a car in Washington, so instead of my having to wait for three hours between trains, he offered me a ride down to Richmond. Wasn't that dear of him?"

Paul and Sam were just the beginning. Every morning Auntie Ethel received calls from new men whom she'd met at parties the night before. I usually answered the phone and said, "Please call later," because she always slept 'til noon.

"That's what vacation is for," she told me when she woke up, sipped her first cup of coffee, and lit a cigarette. "Night time is for parties; day-time is for sleeping."

"Oh, tell me about the parties," I would beseech at these noon-time chats.

Then Auntie Ethel described the beautiful dresses worn by the "girls," and would tell me about the "fellows" with whom she danced until dawn.

Whenever Mother asked her how she liked her date – whoever the date may have been – she would smile and say, "A nice *fel*low," with the accent on the first syllable.

Sometimes a dozen fellows would call Auntie Ethel in one day, and I'd get to take all the messages. "No, you mustn't say she's taking a bubble-bath," Auntie Ethel would call from the tub, "Just say, she's indisposed at the moment."

She always had me tell them to call back about five o'clock. "That's a nice time of day to talk with the fellows," she'd laugh while applying bright red polish to her nails.

I never tired of helping Auntie Ethel dress for her dates. "Now should it be this green thing, or should it be the red print?" she'd ask me, stepping into her three inch heels which made her nearly as tall as Mother, who was five foot five in stocking feet.

Sometimes Daddy brought a new fellow home from the base to meet her. "The Navy's much better," Daddy would tease her. She was always delightfully charming to the lucky fellow, but the next morning when I'd tell him she couldn't talk until five o'clock he sounded as unhappy as the rest of them. Mother told me privately that Grandma hoped Auntie Ethel would meet someone and settle down. "She's nearly thirty now, and Grandma's worried that she won't get married."

I couldn't imagine why Auntie Ethel would want to get married and stop going to parties all the time. One noon, while she sat sipping her coffee and blowing circles of smoke, I asked her. "Well," she said, thinking my question over very seriously, "there are so many swell fellows around that I'd just hate to miss meeting any. So I prefer to play the field. But I know Mama is worried about me. And, Papa wanted me to marry that phewy," she held her nose and made a face, "dentist. So I just came out here for a visit to get away from all that. As long as there are so many new fellows around, why should I get married?"

The Montcastles lived next door to us. Auntie Ethel and Mrs. Montcastle became such good friends that Auntie Ethel soon started talking like a southerner. The Montcastle children were older than me, so I hardly ever saw them. Auntie Ethel told me they insisted on calling her "Ma' am," as all southern children called their teachers and their mothers' friends.

"I told them calling me ma'am is an insult. Ma'am," she scoffed, twirling around the room, her skirt swirling, "Ma'am is for old ladies with white hair."

One day Auntie Ethel came home with the news that the Montcastle children had the measles. "You didn't go near them did you?" Mother asked her.

"I felt sorry for them: I played with them all afternoon," Auntie Ethel said.

"But, Ethel, you haven't had the measles," Mother said.

"Never, and I don't intend to get them," she laughed.

But Mother was worried. Daddy was due for a transfer again; rumor was that he would be shipped out. "Ralph won't want me to get left here with two sick kids; I won't be able to travel if they have measles."

The next day Auntie Ethel started packing her things. "I have to leave in ten days anyway, to go home and get ready for school," she told me. "If I wait and get the measles, then you kids will probably get them from me, and I'll feel terrible. If I go now then there's no worry for your parents."

Auntie Ethel left under military escort. "I can't hurt any of the fellows' feelings," she said, "so I just told them all they could come down to the station."

The Army was on her left, the Navy on her right. The fellows argued over who would carry what for her. She even let one of them carry her purse.

I started to cry when Auntie Ethel kissed me goodbye. But, she had a cure all planned. "Oh, Lolly," she said, "I nearly forgot," as she opened her purse, took her bottle of bright red nail polish from it, and handed it to me. "I think you're old enough to put this on yourself now." And with a laugh she was off. "Take good care of all the fellows," she waved. "And if the war's not over, I'll be back to visit y'all next summer."

Chapter Six
Norfolk – Winter 1944

The rumors were true. Daddy was transferred. But he wasn't shipped out. "We're staying in Virginia. I'll be stationed at the Portsmouth Naval Hospital, but there's no housing there so we'll live across the bay in Norfolk. For now we'll be staying in a small apartment above a barber shop," he told us.

Shrill, blaring noises woke me one of our first nights there. Mother ran in, sat on my bed shshshshing my cries and whispered, "Please don't wake Ricky."

"But what's wrong?" I tried to whisper.

"It's an air raid siren."

What's an air raid?"

"It means enemy planes could be in the area but I think it's just an air raid drill. We were told these drills would sometimes happen in Norfolk."

The sirens kept on and on. "Come," she whispered, "let's sit by the window in my room. I'll lift the shade just a little so we can peek out."

Daddy had overnight duty so I felt extra grown up sitting there alone so late with mother. It felt cozy and safe in spite of the sirens. But there was nothing to see. Everything was black dark. No street lights, no building lights, not anything anywhere.

Soon Daddy got us a 'sub-let' where there were still air raid drills but it was so scary there anyway that I don't remember being awakened again by the sirens. The tall beige house was mostly covered by thin trees with no leaves.

Inside everything was dark brown: the walls, the floors, the chairs, all dark brown. The steep winding front hall staircase with its skinny little banister led to the even darker upstairs.

Every step had its own creaky sound. All the upstairs doors squeaked and creaked. It was terrifying up there when it started getting dark outside, and worse still at 5 o'clock every day when the radio gong sounded for Terry and the Pirates and the melodic voice of that horrid Tokyo Rose came on the air. I shivered and quivered through the whole program and by the time it was over, I was shaking too much to go downstairs to Mother. Instead I'd call down to her on some pretext or other and breathe a huge sigh of relief when she came into my room and the world was all right again.

A wonderful thing happened when we lived in that house, though. I got to go to school. Mother and Daddy started arguing about it a few weeks after we moved in. "Ralph, I found out that in Norfolk children can start first grade mid-year. James Monroe School is nearby; I called and they said since Arlene turns six in January she is welcome to begin One Low right after New Years."

"Geeze, Bea you can't do that." Daddy told her. "You've got to look ahead. Schools are full of germs; she'll get sick all the time, Ricky will catch everything, and I might be shipped out in the midst of it. Then you'll be left alone with sick kids in a strange place. Just leave her be; she can go to school after the war's over."

"*You* think ahead," Mother countered. "Do you want her in first grade when she's nine or ten? Ralph, she needs to be with other children; she doesn't have any children her age to play with because they're all in school."

Thankfully Mother prevailed. She was right; I loved school. Mrs. Pate was the best first grade teacher anybody could ever have imagined: warm, motherly and, though I remember other children being there, it felt like I was her only student. Thanks to the thousands of hours my elocution-trained Mother had spent reading to me I took to phonics immediately, and learned to read right away. It's a good thing because Daddy was right too. Within a short time I got sick. I always had to stay in bed when sneezing, or coughing and fevered. Plus Daddy made me stay home one extra normal temperature day for every day I had a fever. Then back in school a week or so and then the next bug. All in all, I was home much more than in school but it didn't really matter.

By March Mrs. Pate started a contest and whoever read the most books by the last day of school would be the prizewinner. Of course, I won. Nobody else was home with so much time to read. I read all the first grade books and was well into the second grade by year's end when I missed the whole last week of school too. Mrs. Pate came to our house with my prize—-a big box of candy. When I hugged her good-bye I thought she'd be my teacher again in the fall.

But it turned out our sub-let was up and the next house Daddy could get was in the Larchmont school district. It was a perfect house. Not a creepy house, or a plantation or a white cottage but just a middlesize house-house on Rolf Avenue. Larchmont School was just a few blocks away and my One High teacher was Miss Ivey. She was short and pretty with black curls and violet eyes.

There were no germs in that school. I caught them and took them home: Chicken pox, measles, viruses of every variety. I brought them all home and shared generously with Ricky, in spite of Mother using the guest room as a "sick room" to which I was sent from the bedroom Ricky and I shared, at first sign of cough or sneeze.

It was a small bright room at the top of the stairs with a high bed, white sheets and white walls. There were also white filmy curtains on the two big windows which overlooked our back yard with the magnolia tree and gardenia bushes. Each time I moved in sick, it was with a radio to which I listened all day to soaps: *Oxydol's Own Ma Perkins, Our Gal Sunday, The Strange Romance of Helen Trent*. I'd read or draw pictures while I listened and often would doze off in the mid-afternoon during some of the boring ones like *Just Plain Bill*, so as to be well rested by five o'clock when *Hop Harrigan* and *Terry and the Pirates* came on. Tokyo Rose wasn't nearly as scary in that house.

One day when I *was* in school, Miss Ivey answered a knock on the door of our room. She stood there talking for a long time. Then she came back into the room, walked to my desk and said "Arlene, you have a visitor. You may go out into the hall."

Who would visit me? Mother and Ricky walked me as far as the school patrol every morning but they never came to visit during the day. Daddy was at the Hospital. There was nobody else. I walked uncertainly to the door.

The soldier standing there grabbed me and threw me up into the air. "There's a moose in the hoose, get it oot!" The line that had me laughing ever since I could remember.

I could not believe it. It was Uncle Manuel. "But, Uncle Manuel you're in the South Pacific."

"The H—-I am! I'm right here in Norfolk. I talked to your teacher and you can come home with me now. I told your mother I would come up and get you out of class and take you back to your house. She said I couldn't; that it's against the rules. But I sweet-talked that teacher of yours. She's a real looker. She said when your Uncle who you haven't seen in over two years comes to town she guesses it's okay for you to leave early with him."

"Uncle Manuel, how long can you stay?"

"I wouldn't stay for ten minutes in this God-forsaken town if you all weren't here," he answered. "But the Army sent me to Norfolk and I'm not going to tell them I have a brother here. The Army and Navy try not to station brothers in the same place in case of bombing. I'll be glad to stay as long as you all are here."

For the first two months he was in Norfolk, Uncle Manuel had funny hours. He was off during the afternoons, then on duty at night. So he came to school to get me very often. He usually came early and waited until school was out. Whenever he did, Miss Ivey had us put down our *Dick and Jane* readers even if we were in the middle of a good story. Then she stayed out in the hall talking to Uncle Manuel while she had us work on penmanship. As much as I loved having Uncle Manuel come to school, I hated penmanship so much that I didn't even mind when he got switched to day duty.

Chapter Seven
A Real Neighborhood – Summer 1944

On Rolf Avenue Mother's dream of our living in a real neighborhood finally came true. For the first time ever we lived with other families all around us complete with playmates for Ricky and me.

Carolyn's house was just behind ours, Janie's and Dale's houses were right across the street, Jonny and Ginny Lou's house was kitty-corner from ours. There was always somebody to play with and there were neighborhood parties, too. Birthday parties were lots of fun with ice cream and cake, playing pin the tail on the donkey, and sometimes bobbing for apples, which I only watched but never did. Even Mother said there were too many germs.

Neighborhood birthday party, Norfolk spring 1945: Ricky second from left; me back row far right, bow in hair, eyes closed

"Going out Halloweening" was the best. One year Mother made me a clown costume; another Halloween I got to be a gypsy wearing Mother's jewelry and even her lipstick and rouge. Every family had its trick-and-treat specialties: at Jonny and Ginny Lou's we were given huge caramel popcorn balls, at Janie's big chocolate chip cookies and at ours Halloween cupcakes for which Mother saved ration points all month.

What fun to watch Mother stand intently at the sink mixing the yellow and red food coloring in order to make the frosting come out a rich pumpkin-colored orange. Oh, she'd get so mad if she couldn't make it come out just right on the first try. Ricky and I got to frost the cupcakes and decorate each face using corn candy for noses, maraschino cherries for mouths and raisins for eyes.

Many of the families were military like ours. Janie's father was gone for months at a time on the ship he commanded; so was Dale's. Other families like Pebby's were Virginians. Pebby (Mrs. Pebworth to me) came over the very first day we arrived with a plate of oatmeal cookies and said, "Bill and I have lived on this street for over thirty years and raised our children here. I'm right next door, please stop in often."

I don't know if Mother and Ricky went to Pebby's when I was at school, but Pebby sat talking to Mother and drinking coffee at our kitchen table a lot. One afternoon when Pebby was there, I answered the phone. It was the minister who lived down the block, asking to talk to Mother. That was funny. He and his wife were the only unfriendly people in our neighborhood. They never talked to us if they could help it, and they didn't let their little girl play with Ricky and me either. So why would he be calling?

"Mother, it's the Reverend," I told her. She excused herself and went to the phone, shutting the sunroom door behind her. When she came out a few minutes later she headed back to Pebby and exploded. "He needs to keep his nose out of other peoples' business. Can you imagine, Pebby, he said that here in Virginia white children do not play with colored children. He said it was '…inexcusable that I allowed a colored child here today and that it should never happen again.'"

Oh so that was why he called up. He didn't like Leah's pretty dark skin. Sometimes Leah's mother, Naomi came to help Mother clean. Weeks ago, Mother asked Naomi to bring Leah with her today, since it was vacation and Leah and I are both seven. We had a good time; first we played inside with my jewelry-making kit and then we went out in front and played with her jacks, and hop-scotched on the sidewalk and then jumped rope.

At first Pebby, who usually talked a lot, didn't say anything. "Pebby, I have a perfect right to invite whom I wish, don't I?" Mother asked her.

"Well, of course you do," Pebby said, "but you know Bea, he is young. Perhaps he meant to say that here white folks don't have much occasion to socialize with colored folks," to which Mother replied, "Well then, we'll just have to create more such occasions."

Chapter Eight
The Paraplane Kit – Spring 1945

I ate Wheaties for breakfast for nearly a month. As soon as I opened the third Wheaties box, I sent for my Hop Harrigan paraplane kit. But Mother made me eat all the Wheaties in the box anyway.

For weeks, I dreamed of flying my Hop Harrigan paraplane just like Hop did when I listened to him on the bedroom radio every afternoon at five o'clock. Now I had the paraplane kit in my hands. What to do with it was another matter. On the radio they said the directions were simple. But there was nothing easy about these instructions. Mother couldn't figure out how to make the plane fly either. Daddy had overnight duty so he wasn't home.

When I got to school the next morning, I couldn't believe that Charles Mitchell, the tallest, most well-liked boy in the class, was sitting at my desk. He was talking to the next most well-liked boy, Charles Eby, who sat behind me. I kept the two Charles' straight by thinking of them as yellow Charles and brown Charles. Charles Mitchell was blonde, blue-eyed and freckled, while Charles Eby had dark hair and eyes like mine. Charles Eby sometimes talked to me during silent reading but Charles Mitchell had never talked to me before.

"Let me keep your seat another minute," Charles Mitchell said, hardly looking up. "This is really important.

It was important. Charles Mitchell and Charles Eby were putting together a Hop Harrigan paraplane. "We'll be done in another second," Charles Eby said.

"That's okay, but can I watch? My paraplane came yesterday but it won't go together right."

"That's girls," Charles Mitchell said. "It's cinchy, you were probably doing it all wrong. I got mine together in two minutes yesterday and now we've got his done, too. We're going to fly them at recess."

"I wish mine would fly," I said.

"It will," Charles Mitchell said masterfully. "I'll come over after school. In fact, we both will, won't we Chuck?" he asked Charles Eby.

"I guess we can," Charles Eby said.

"We'll put yours together and then we'll all race our planes," Charles Mitchell said, "Okay?"

"Okay", I said, hoping he couldn't tell how excited I was. Imagine me, getting to go with the boys after school. And not just any boys, but the two nicest boys in the class. Usually the Charles' played ball after school on the playground with some of the other boys. Usually I walked home with Carolyn Holmes who lived behind us, or Ginny Lou Herger who lived down the street.

But today I walked home from school between Charles Mitchell and Charles Eby. I waved to Carolyn and Ginny

Lou as we hurried by. Red-ringleted Kay White, who always teased me about being fat said "Hi." But I just kept walking.

When we got home, Mother gave us orange juice and chocolate chip cookies. "Thank you Ma'am," the boys said before they ate, and "Thank you again, Ma'am," when they were finished.

I brought my paraplane to the kitchen table. "See," I said, "I fit all the pieces together but it still won't fly."

Charles Mitchell took it all apart. Then he put it back together, but it still wouldn't fly. "Something's missing," he said. "No wonder it won't fly. Have you ever heard of a plane flying on only one wing?"

"But the wing goes all across," I said.

"It's still only one wing," he answered. "Look at mine, and at Chuck's. We have two of those long wings."

He was right. My plane was missing a wing.

"How many boxtops did you send in?" Charles Mitchell asked me.

"Three like it said," I told him.

"Only three? I sent four. You were supposed to send four," said Charles Eby.

I was sure it said three. So that was why they didn't send me the whole plane. I hadn't eaten enough Wheaties.

"I'm going to have to send for another plane," I said, "But it's another month of Wheaties."

"I'll tell you what," Charles Mitchell said. "If you give us this plane to use for spare parts, you can fly our planes with us until yours comes. Is that a deal?"

Was that a deal?

I got to fly planes at recess with Charles and Charles on the boys' side of the playground. Sometimes I caught sight of Carolyn and Ginny Lou looking up enviously from their jacks game on the girls side. Kay White never teased me about being fat anymore and she always said "hi" first. I kept eating Wheaties for breakfast, but the offer expired before I ate enough of them.

It didn't matter, though. Charles Mitchell and Charles Eby soon tired of their paraplanes. "Boring," Charles Mitchell said. "Yeah, boring," echoed Charles Eby. "We're sending for Terry and the Pirates special decoding kits," Charles Eby confided to me one day during reading.

I'd been thinking about doing that myself. "How many?" I asked him.

"Three Rice Krispie boxtops plus a quarter."

I switched to Rice Krispies the next day. When the decoding set came all the parts were there.

Chapter Nine
The Hurricane – April 1945

It was windy and raining when I got up. "Maybe you'd better not go to school today," Mother said. "A hurricane is supposed to be headed this way."

"Oh, no...please don't make me stay home." I'd never heard of a hurricane. And there was so much to do in Miss Epes' second grade that I hated ever to miss school.

Mother finally gave in to my pleas, aided no doubt by the knowledge that if I did stay home with nothing to do I'd fight with Ricky.

The sky was dark. Charles Eby and Charles Mitchell took turns running to the window and bringing back reports. "It's really raining hard...the wind is terrible..."

None of us could concentrate on our spelling. Finally Miss Epes said, "Please get your air raid rugs out from under your desks."

We had air-raid drills every couple of weeks. At the sound of the continually ringing school bell, we immediately stopped whatever we were doing, ran for our rugs, and lay down on them while Miss Epes pulled the shades, and turned out the lights.

Now, would we have a hurricane drill?

"If the hurricane strikes, you're best down low," Miss Epes said. "Now we'll take our rugs down to the lunchroom, and practice just what we'll do, if the hurricane comes."

We lay on our rugs giggling.

Charles Eby tickled Charles Mitchell. He yelled.

Miss Epes suggested we sing some songs. We each got to pick.

Charles Mitchell wanted *Five Little Drums*.

Charles Eby chose *Anchors Aweigh*. Kay White asked for *Susie Little Susie*; the boys groaned but Miss Epes said they had to join in.

I picked *The Erie Canal* so we could do a lot of sound effects.

After singing we walked up to our classrooms. Several mothers were waiting outside the door.

"Are you here to take your children home?" Miss Epes asked.

"Yes," one of them answered. As if it were a signal, more and more mothers started arriving. Kay White's mother came. Mrs. Mitchell came and took her Charles, and also Charles Eby. Pretty soon only the James twins and I were left. Then their mother came.

Why, oh why, didn't my mother come? She walked me to the school patrol when nobody else's mother did. She always picked me up at the school door when it was raining. Hardly anybody else's mother did. So why, now, was she leaving me at school during a hurricane?

"Can I please call my Mother?" I asked Miss Epes.

"Yes, I think that's a good idea," she told me. "Take this pass to the office and ask to use the telephone for a minute."

I dialed 23781 but there was no answer. I dialed again. She must be on the way.

I went back to the room but still no Mother. Miss Ivey stopped at the door, "Are you ready to leave, Vi?" she asked Miss Epes.

"I still have a student," Miss Epes said. "You go ahead. I'll get a ride with someone else."

"There's hardly anybody else left," Miss Ivey told her.

Just then Mother came running into the room. Her beige raincoat and rainhat were dripping wet.

"My goodness, Miss Epes, I'm so sorry," she said. "I wanted to come as soon as the storm began but my husband called twice and told me he thought that Arlene would be safer here, because it's such a big heavy building."

"He's right," Miss Epes said, "except most of the parents prefer to come for the children, feeling that they'll be frightened of staying here."

"Well, I'll be happier to have her with me," Mother said. "I've been nervous all morning and finally I decided I'd come for her in spite of her father's concerns."

We blew home. There were very few cars on the streets. Mother navigated ours through huge pools of water. "I left Ricky next door with Pebby," she said. "Pebby's lived here all her life and has been through many hurricanes. She agreed with your father that you'd be safer in school, but I was afraid you could be stranded there for the night, and maybe longer."

We took Ricky from Pebby's. Mother had to carry her up the front steps of the house because the water was so high.

"Remember," Pebby warned, "the staircase is your safest place."

So we went inside and sat on our staircase. Mother made us sandwiches and we ate them on the third step. By lunchtime the water was seeping into the living room; and the wind was howling fiercely. Later in the afternoon Mother made more sandwiches; we ate them on the landing.

"I wonder how your father is?" Mother said. "He hasn't called for the last three hours."

A few minutes later, we heard the front door open; the wind must have blown it in. I peeked around the landing.

It was not the wind. It was Daddy. He was drenched! "Where is everybody?" he called as he rushed up to the landing.

"How on earth did you get here?" Mother asked.

"The Captain's gig."

"What do you mean the Captain's gig? I thought you had the Duty and wouldn't be back until tomorrow."

"That's right. But then I called and you weren't here and I got worried. I wanted to make sure you were all right here and that Lolly was okay at school, but I see you've got her."

"How did you arrange with the Captain to get his yacht?"

"I didn't exactly arrange it with the Captain. But, I know a young sailor who has run the gig for the Captain and he, ah, agreed to borrow it long enough to run me across the river. He's got it tied up now at the river about four blocks from here. It's tied to a tree, but I don't know how long the tree's going to last, so I've got to get right back."

"You stole the Captain's gig? You're going to wind up in the brig!" Mother shouted in alarm.

"He stole the gig, he's in the brig," Ricky and I chimed in.

"It took us about half hour across," Daddy said. "Boy, was that some ride," he told us. "My stomach's still out there in Chesapeake Bay. If we're lucky and get back as fast as we got here, we'll be gone not much over an hour. The Captain's a very sensible man. He wouldn't be looking to go for a boat ride in the midst of a hurricane; he won't miss it."

Daddy wrapped some dry clothes in a towel and put them in a canvas bag along with some apples. "In case we're shipwrecked and hungry," he laughed.

"Now, stay in, don't go near any windows, or doors," he commanded as he kissed us all and then ran back outside to take a boat-ride in the hurricane.

"Promise to call me the minute to you get back!" Mother shouted after him as he disappeared into the wind and rain.

Mother read us stories while we waited. She had to read really loudly so we could hear her over the howling wind. Between stories she went to the window. Each time she came back she shook her head, but she didn't mention Daddy. I didn't either but I was thinking about him.

Mother read the whole week's library books and then started on our own books. She read all our favorite Pooh chapters and about Kanga getting lost twice. We were partway through *The Little Princess* when the phone finally rang.

I got to it first. "Hi, kid," Daddy said calmly. "You all okay?" I started to ask him if the waves were high but

Mother grabbed the phone. When she got off she was smiling.

It's a good thing Daddy called when he did. A half hour later our phone line went dead. It didn't work again for a week.

Chapter Ten
The Plant – May 1945

During the sunny second week of May Mother and Ricky didn't walk me to the school patrol crossing as they usually did, because Mother had pneumonia. The doctors wanted her to go to the hospital but there were no beds. The hospital was filled with sick and wounded sailors. Daddy was very worried about her, but he felt she was better off at home. He knew too much about hospitals and he didn't trust them.

He found a lady named Mrs. Casserly to take care of Mother and Ricky. I went to school and took care of myself.

On the Friday afternoon before Mother's Day, there was a Mother's Day Bazaar at school. That meant everyone got to go down to the lunchroom and buy presents. The rooms were called one by one.

When our room's turn came I was very excited. I knew that a present would help make Mother better. And she had to get better soon. Just yesterday Daddy started her on a new medicine. It was very hard to get because it was brand new and reserved for the Army and Navy personnel. But after days of arguing Daddy managed to convince the Navy that he had to have some for Mother. The big pills looked awful. They were called Sulpha.

Poor Mother had to stay in bed and take terrible looking medicine. But, I could find something at the Bazaar to make her better. What would it be? The lunchroom tables were laden with beautiful handkerchiefs, pretty scarves, bright green plants...I wanted to buy one of everything. But I only had a dime. I'd meant to ask Daddy for some money. He always gave me money when I needed it. He had lots of nickels, dimes and quarters in his pockets which he emptied out on the dresser at night. If I needed a nickel he held out a hand full of change and said, "take more, kid...take as much as you want." But I only ever took what I needed.

If I'd remembered about the Bazaar and asked him this morning he would have given me lots and lots of coins. He'd have said, "Here, kid, buy something from me, and from Ricky, too." But, he and another doctor were examining Mother when I left for school and I just waved goodbye and forgot all about the Bazaar.

Now, what would I do? Almost everything on the overflowing table cost more than a dime. The only things I saw which cost a dime were some tiny little earrings and Mother never wore earrings.

Miss Epes blew her whistle, "Come here, we have to make room for the next class...if you're in line now to pay you may stay and finish. Otherwise, come back to the room. If you haven't made your purchases you may return to do so after school."

I thought about the earrings all through arithmetic. Maybe Mother would start wearing earrings. Maybe it would make her feel better just to look at earrings and think about where she might wear them. I knew in my heart she would like the yellow-embroidered hanky better, but it cost 20 cents. She would love the red and blue scarf, but that was 35 cents. She would get better right away from the beautiful big green plant but it cost 50 cents. Even if I had 50 cents it would be too big to carry home.

As soon as the bell rang I grabbed my sweater and books and ran down to the lunchroom. It was almost empty, and the earrings were gone. I looked at the rest of the hankies. The prettiest ones were gone and the others still cost more than a dime. There were only two scarves left, and they each cost a quarter. All the big plants were gone. There were only a few plants left, and every one of them cost more than a dime. I stood by the plants and started to cry. How could I have forgotten about the Bazaar and come without enough money? Now Mother would never get better.

"What's wrong?" a big girl in a plaid skirt asked me. I had seen her before; she was in the fourth grade.

"I don't have enough money to buy my Mother a present and she is sick besides," I told her between sniffles.

"Just a minute," she said, "wait right there."

She came back with a lady who I'd seen standing at the money table where the kids paid for the presents. "Can I help you?" the lady asked me, handing me a kleenex.

I told her what was wrong.

"Well, I think we can do something about this," she said kindly. "We're going to mark down the plants we haven't sold so that we don't have to take them all home again. Why don't you pick out whichever plant you would like and then bring me your dime and I'll wrap the plant for you."

I could have kissed her. All of the plants were pretty. It was hard to decide. Finally I took one with a purple flower.

It was the smallest of the plants but the purple flower reminded me of the flowers Mother and I used to walk through in Hastings when I was little. This plant would surely make her better.

I usually left school at 2:15, but now it was 2:45. I would have to hurry. No use for Mother to worry about me when she was sick. The patrols were all gone and there were no other kids around. I started walking fast. I was careful at every crossing, and looked to the left and then to the right. But, it was a long, lonesome walk. And, besides, I had to go to the bathroom. Badly. In fact, by the time I got to the block before ours I had to go very badly. So badly that I started running but that made it worse. I had to walk slowly with one leg crossing over the other. But finally that stopped helping, too.

By the time I got to the front door, I didn't have to go anymore. I rushed into Mother's room. She was sitting up in bed for the first time in a week. "What happened? Why are you so late?"

"I tried and tried to buy you a Mother's Day present at the Bazaar to make you better but I didn't have enough money, and so I had to stay after and go look again and then finally the plant cost less so I could buy it, but, then I was late and I had to hurry and there were no patrols and then I had to go to the bathroom so badly and there wasn't any and so, and so...."

Mother looked down at my legs and socks. She laughed for the first time in a week. “Go and get washed and changed right away,” she said. “Then come back in and we’ll unwrap the plant together. I know I’m going to love it. It’s made me much better already.”

Chapter Eleven
Summertime – July 1945

School was out and so was I. Daddy didn't allow me to play inside the house with other kids. It was polio season.

When I heard Daddy put the needles in the kettle to sterilize them, I decided to run away. The gamma globulin shots hurt and meant a big red welt on my leg for a week.

"It only hurts for a minute, kid," Daddy said, "and it's a lot better than getting polio."

Daddy had specialized in pediatrics but switched to psychiatry and neurology because he couldn't stand seeing children die or become paralyzed from polio. At Hastings he used to have incubators filled with chick embryos on which he did polio research. He believed that gamma globulin, a composite of blood taken from adults who had already survived numerous polio epidemics, would help prevent polio. "At least it might prevent the crippling complications," he said.

When the neighbors heard that Daddy gave Ricky and me some kind of shots against polio, they asked if he would give shots to their children, too. He said that he would.

Now the needles were boiling, and in a little while Mrs. Gibbony from down the block would bring Helen, and Mrs. Holmes from across the backyard would bring Carolyn, and Mrs. Herger from around the corner would bring Jonny and Ginny Lou. Our kitchen would become a clinic as everyone of them got a shot. But, I wouldn't be there for my shot. I was running away. I took the smallest of my suitcases from the back of my closet and put some clothes in it. I packed a blanket and "pillowese," my small pillow which had been on my bed in Hastings ever since I moved from the crib to the junior bed. I took my copy of *Primrose Day* and a stack of *Patsy Walker* comic books. What about food? I'd like some cookies. But, if I went into the kitchen I might be discovered. I couldn't risk it. I'd have to leave with no food.

Arlene (incognito) getting ready to run away

It was hot and humid. Where would I go? I thought of hiding under the back steps where it was cool and shaded. But I might be discovered there. Jonny Herger would probably bring his cat and the cat would crawl under to get cool and then Jonny would find me.

I headed off to the corner...the opposite direction from the Hergers and the Holmes. Around that corner and halfway down the block there was a big house; I don't know who lived there. But they had a huge magnolia tree which shaded most of the sidewalk. That would be as good a place as any to hide out. I spread my blanket, put pillowese on it and lay down. It was pleasant and safe. Nobody would look for me here. I finished *Primrose Day* and read half of my comics when Daddy said, "Oh, here you are, kid. I was looking for you. I'm glad you got out of the house. I had Mother keep Ricky upstairs while the others were there. I didn't want you two exposed to the other kids."

He didn't seem to understand that I had run away. "Here, let me help you get your things together," he said.

I didn't want to mention that I was running away because if I ran away again then he'd know exactly where to look for me.

"Come on," he said, taking me by the hand. "We'll get your shot over with and then let's put the hammock out between our trees in the backyard. Then you'll have a shady place to read without having to come down the block."

Chapter Twelve
The Phone Call – August 1945

Auntie Ethel did not come to visit again the next summer as she promised. And she didn't come the next summer either. Instead, she got married.

After she left Richmond, she found Minneapolis too boring. The fellows were either away in service, too old, or too sickly to go. Now that she'd given the Army and Navy on the east coast a chance she thought she'd try the west. "I'm going to live with Cousin Jeannette and teach in L.A. for a while," she wrote cheerily.

Her letters were glowing. There were many more fellows to go with and even more parties to go to in Los Angeles than in Richmond. That had to be a lot. Then, one night Auntie Ethel met Lew Perlman. He was already discharged from the service and working for a movie studio. Two weeks later she decided to marry him.

Grandma and Grandpa took the train from Minneapolis to Los Angeles for the wedding. Uncle Mel took the train there from Washington. But Mother couldn't go because she had to stay in Norfolk and take care of us.

Mother cried the morning of the wedding. "If I could only talk to my sister and wish her luck," she said. "But I can't get a call through."

The wedding was to take place at two o'clock, Los Angeles time. It was now one o'clock our time—we were three hours ahead. Mother had been trying, without success to get a call through for over two hours. Daddy tried, too, but he couldn't either. The only calls which could be made to civilians were those of emergency, meaning family death or severe illness. No long distance calls for happy reasons. This was war time.

The front screen door banged open and a familiar voice sang out, "The coffee in the Army, they say it's mighty fine; it's good for cuts and bruises and it tastes like iodine...."

Uncle Manuel. I ran to the door. "Are you off duty all day?"

"I sure am and boy, baby, I want to take you to the Officer's Club. There's a huge pool, and a cabana, and lots of good food."

I wanted to go badly. Uncle Manuel kept asking and asking us all summer. It sounded like fun. A cabana—whatever it was—sounded glamorous.

"You know Daddy won't let us go anywhere because of polio."

"You aren't going to get any polio when you're with your Uncle Manuel... hey, what's this? What are you crying about, Bea?"

"Shhh," Daddy said. "Leave her alone, Manuel. She's real upset. Ethel's getting married in a couple of hours and we haven't been able to get a call through to her. Bea feels awful; the rest of the family is all gathered there and here she's four thousand miles away and can't even wish Ethel good luck by phone...

"Oh, hell, is that all that's the matter? I can fix that, easy," Uncle Manuel said.

"Manuel, you're just full of talk. It can't be done," Mother told him.

"What will you bet me? Huh? What will you do if I get the call through?"

"Nothing, because you can't do it."

"If I get that call through to Ethel then you, Ralph, and the girls will come with me to the Officers' Club...we'll sit by the pool, and maybe swim. And we'll have some good food there...okay?"

He looked from Mother to Daddy.. . "Agreed? Okay?"

Daddy held the phone out to his younger brother. "Go on, just make the call."

Ricky and I ran to get our bathing suits. "Just a minute," Daddy warned. "He doesn't even have an operator on the line, yet."

Uncle Manuel soon did have a line for the operator. "Hello, Baby," he said softly into the telephone. "I've got a real emergency and I need all the help you can give me....." He talked softly into the phone and we couldn't hear the rest, but it was probably like whatever he used to say to Miss Ivey in the hall outside our classroom. Whatever it was, shortly Uncle Manuel called, "Hey, Bea, what's Ethel's phone number?" Mother quickly gave him a piece of paper with the number, which he read to the operator. "Okay, baby," he said into the phone, "I'll wait right here by the phone. Remember, I'm counting on you.

It seemed like an hour but it was only ten minutes until our phone rang. Uncle Manuel answered. "Yes, operator, we're waiting on the call...Ethel congratulations! It's Manuel. Bea wants to talk to you...here's the phone, Bea."

"Ethel, Ethel, you sound like you're in the next room," Mother said.

Daddy and Uncle Manuel shooed Ricky and me out of the den so Mother could talk without interruption. She talked to Auntie Ethel and Grandma and Grandpa. When she came out of the den she was crying again. But she was smiling, too. "What are you waiting for?" she sniffled, "Let's put on our bathing suits and get to the pool."

The Officers' Club was even more wonderful than I'd imagined. It was a big white building with columns, and there were buffet tables of food all around. The pool was huge. We got to stay all afternoon and Daddy even let us get our feet wet in the pool, although he wouldn't let us go in. It didn't matter, though. It was exciting to finally get to go there, and it seemed as if we were celebrating Auntie Ethel's wedding after all.

Chapter Thirteen
Going Home – April 1946

The war was over. We won. Everybody was excited. There would be no more fighting and killing. Soldiers and sailors could go home. The Star-Spangled Banner blared over the radio; the newspapers showed pictures of people throwing confetti and dancing in the streets. Everybody was happy. Everybody but me.

I didn't want to go back to Hastings. That was long ago and far away. Norfolk was my home now; Larchmont was my school. Carolyn and Ginny Lou and Helen and Barbara and Charles and Charles were my friends. Why, oh why, did we have to leave Norfolk? Why couldn't we stay? Uncle Manuel was staying.

One night when Mother and Daddy were packing, I answered the door and there was Uncle Manuel with a small, dark-haired woman. She wore a yellow rain-slicker. He had his arm around her and he did not even try to pick me up, much less sing.

"Hey, aren't you going to invite your uncle and your almost-aunt Clara in?" he asked.

"What's an almost-aunt Clara?" I asked, as I moved aside so they could come in. But I figured that it had to do with this short, quiet woman standing there with him.

As soon as he and Clara and Mother and Daddy all came into the living room, he announced, "Clara and I are getting married. I'm going to stay here and work in her family's furniture store. So, you'll always have a home to come to in Norfolk even when you go back to Minnesota."

"But Uncle Manuel, you said you wouldn't stay in this town ten minutes if we weren't here, remember you said it the first day you came to get me at school?" I reminded him.

"Did I say a thing like that?" he asked me, smiling down at Clara.

"Maybe I could stay in Norfolk with you," I hinted, "and never go back to Minnesota either." But he didn't seem to hear me.

Anyway, even if I did stay and live with them I would miss Mother and Daddy and never get to see Grandma and Grandpa.

Mother and Daddy could not stay in Norfolk.

"Kid," Daddy said, "You know that I'm on leave of absence from the State of Minnesota. I've got eleven hundred patients waiting for me. I need to get back to Hastings. Your mother needs to get back to her folks and I need to get back to my mother."

We packed up all our things. The house was very empty.

I said goodbye to all my friends at school one afternoon. It turned out that I wasn't the only one leaving.

"We're going back to Indiana next week," Charles Eby told me.

Lt. Commander Dr. Ralph Rossen, Ricky and Arlene leaving Norfolk

When I said goodbye to Mrs. Harper she said, "I'm sorry to lose you, and you're only the first. Half the class will be gone before the school year is over."

Later that afternoon I said goodbye to the neighbor kids.

"Dad just got his mustering out papers yesterday," Ginny Lou said, "We're going back to Georgia next month."

Still I didn't want to leave. Hastings was a long, long time ago. I was no longer a princess in a castle; I was just a regular person in a regular house like everybody else. That's what I was thinking about as I sat on the front steps of our house that last night.

"I know you're feeling sad about leaving," Daddy said as he came out and stood by our gardenias. "But we're not going someplace new again; we're going home."

"This is home. I don't want to leave," I told him.

Daddy started laughing.

"It's not funny," I said, "How can you laugh?"

"Well, I just happened to think, you could hide your ring again and then we'd have to stay here to find it," he said.

"Daddy," I could feel my face get very hot. "You knew all the time?" I looked at the baby finger of my right hand where I wore the ring now.

"Sure, I did. The ring fit your middle finger so well it couldn't just have fallen off. I knew you were trying to keep me from leaving. Think about it Kid, we've been very, very fortunate you know. Remember how hard it was to leave Hastings that night? We weren't sure if you and Rick and Mother could join me. We didn't know if I'd get shipped out. We didn't know if I'd ever come back."

As Daddy talked, I started to remember things about Hastings I hadn't thought about since we left. I thought about my sled. About the beautiful mountains of fresh white snow. About Frank. About our big house filled with lots and lots of company every weekend. About the big school building in Hastings where we used to go to the library. Now I would go to school there.

The more I thought about Hastings, going back didn't feel so strange after all. Hastings was our real home; Norfolk was our wartime home. But the war was over. For the first time since the war ended I started to feel excited. We were getting to go home: Daddy, Mother, Ricky and me. All together.

"You know what?" I said to Daddy "This is better. This is much better than when you left Hastings. We all got to come with you. You never got sent overseas. Now we all get to go home together." I gave him a big hug and hurried into the house to finish packing my books.

The next morning we piled into our little white Chevrolet coupe and headed for Minnesota. I didn't look back.

Additional Family Photos

Grandpa and Abigail Ora (my Hebrew name by which Grandpa always called me) Hastings, spring 1940

Grandma Mary Witebsky Cohen, Ricky
and Arlene Ora, Hastings, fall 1942

Aunt Minnie Rossen, Libby Rossen, Uncle Manuel and me, Arlene Ora Rossen, summer 1940

Ethabelle Cohen (Auntie Ethel) and
Arlene Ora, Hastings, spring 1940

Virginia Beach, Virginia, Arlene,
Mother and Ricky, summer 1944

Virginia Beach, Virginia, Arlene,
Ricky and Daddy summer 1944

Ricky and Me Waiting to Pick Daddy
up at the ferry from Portsmouth
Naval Hospital, Norfolk 1944